CAREER ANCHORS

THE CHANGING NATURE OF WORK AND CAREERS

PARTICIPANT WORKBOOK

FOURTH EDITION

Edgar H. Schein
John Van Maanen

WILEY

Published by Wiley
One Montgomery Street, Suite 1200, San Francisco, CA 94104-4594
www.wiley.com

For additional copies/bulk purchases of this book in the U.S. please contact 800–274–4434.

Wiley books and products are available through most bookstores. To contact Pfeiffer directly call our Customer Care Department within the U.S. at 800-274-4434, outside the U.S. at 317-572-3985, fax 317-572-4002, or visit www.wiley.com.

Wiley publishes in a variety of print and electronic formats and by print-on-demand. Some material included with standard print versions of this book may not be included in e-books or in print-on-demand. If this book refers to media such as a CD or DVD that is not included in the version you purchased, you may download this material at http://booksupport.wiley.com. For more information about Wiley products, visit www.wiley.com.

ISBN: 978-1-118-45575-3

Acquiring Editor: Holly Allen
Director of Development: Kathleen Dolan Davies
Production Editor: Dawn Kilgore
Editor: Rebecca Taff
Manufacturing Supervisor: Becky Morgan

Printed in the United States of America
Printing   SKY10027362_052721

Contents

Introduction

THE PURPOSE OF THIS WORKBOOK is to give you information about career development, to provide you with a self-reflective process that will enable you to assess more fully your career anchor, and to provide you with a way of analyzing your current job situation as well as possible future career options. To improve the career development process, you must understand fully how careers develop, what role career anchors play in that development, and how career anchors relate to job characteristics.

The *Career Anchors Self-Assessment* that you completed to give yourself a quick, initial picture of your career orientations should now be supplemented by exploring more fully how career anchors develop, how different anchors function, and how they relate to job, family, and personal concerns. To gain more insight into your own situation, this workbook provides you with instructions to do a personal career history, either by yourself in written form or, preferably, with the help of another person who knows you well and will interview you and provide some feedback. (See pages 11 through 17).

Following your career anchor diagnosis, the workbook shows you how to build a Role Map (page 55) to help you to analyze your present career and job situation and assess how well your career anchor is matched to your current job. This section also asks you to consider the issues of role ambiguity, role overload, and role conflict that may be present in your current job and what you might do to resolve them.

The next section of the workbook introduces you to the Work Career and Family/Life Priority Grid to help you think about the kinds of tradeoffs that are involved over time in your career among family, work, and personal commitments (page 64). This section requires considering just how involved you wish or expect to be in your work career now and in the future relative to how much time you wish to spend with others close to you—your partner or others to whom you are closely tied. To place yourself on the grid means assessing how you integrate—or would like to integrate—family and personal responsibilities and commitments with work responsibilities and commitments over time.

The Looking Ahead section that follows (page 71 through 88) takes up where the world of work seems to be going in the future. It asks you to think about some of the changes that are occurring in the workplace, in society, in the world at large. Of course, sorting out trends and predicting what will happen is highly problematic, but some shifts appear more likely than others. The section also provides a look at what the future may have in store for particular career anchors.

The final section of the workbook is called Implications for Your Career Development (page 89). It offers some guidance on how to think about your future in the world of work. The fifty-item survey checklist is provided to help you to assess your current strengths and weaknesses in terms of future job requirements; the checklist will enable you to determine what you need to do in terms of your own personal development.

Career Development

The "Internal Career" and Career Anchors

The word "career" is used in many different ways and has many connotations. Sometimes "having a career" is used to apply only to someone who has a profession or whose occupational life is well structured and involves steady recognition and advancement. But if we think of a career as being what any individual would regard as the steps and phases of his or her occupation, then everyone has a career, and that career is "anchored" by the person's self-image of his or her competencies, motives, and values.

One might consider this to be the "internal career," to distinguish it from what others might view that person's work life to be. Everyone has some kind of picture of his or her work life and role in that life. To distinguish the "internal career" from other uses of the word, we will use "external career" to refer to the actual steps that are required or expected by an occupation or an organization to progress through that occupation. A physician must complete medical school, internship, residency, specialty board examinations, and so on. In some organizations, a general manager has to go through several business functions, have experience in supervising people, take on a functional management job, rotate through the international division, and serve on the corporate staff before being given a true generalist job as a division general manager.

Most external careers involve a period of training or apprenticeship during which the person both learns and is tested to determine whether he or she has the skills and personal characteristics to do the job. Some organizations talk of career paths, which define the necessary or at least desirable steps for the career occupant to take along the way to some goal job. The clearest examples of that kind of formal path are the military and the civil service, with their well-defined ranks, clear rules for how one goes from one rank to another, and the salary levels associated with each level.

At the other extreme is what more and more people are calling a "boundaryless" career or a "protean" career that is more free-form, has to be managed largely by the career occupant, and may involve movements across many employers (Arthur & Rousseau, 1996; Brisoce & Hall 2006; Briscoe, Hall, & Mayrhofer, 2011). Whereas organizations used to promise "employment security," employers are increasingly promising nothing at all or only "employability security," implying that you will learn on-the-job skills that will make you more employable *elsewhere*. Career planning and development programs within organizations—once the province of relatively strong human resources departments—have been trimmed if not eliminated as companies move toward more flexible and "lean" employment policies (Farber, 2008; Harrison, 1997).

Related to this, contract or temporary work is on the rise across most labor markets, including professions and managers, and job tenure in these occupations has been declining precipitously in all developed countries for the past twenty or so years (Barley & Kunda, 2006; Osterman, 2008). More and more people are working part-time at several jobs simultaneously or as short-term contract workers. And most of us today expect to have a serial organizational career rather than a lifetime job with one employer. "Job hopping" is increasingly the norm. One estimate suggests that those who entered the U.S. workforce in 2000 will change employers twelve to fifteen times during their working lives" (Sennett, 2006, p. 95).

These trends—accelerating from the 1980s on—mean far more career instability and uncertainty than in times past. Increasingly, you must manage your own career more and more actively, even if you hope to remain in a single organization. This makes it more important than ever to understand your internal career and the role that career anchors play in it.

External Career Stages and Career Movement

Externally defined career stages are usually well defined by formal occupational criteria and by organizations, if the career is embedded in an organization. Thus, young engineers can pretty well see their external careers in terms of the amount of schooling necessary, entry into an organization as a technical person or management trainee, followed by that organization's specification of how it defines "career development." Most organizations have some career "paths" that are based on historical data of what previous entrants have experienced and can tell the young engineer or manager-to-be what steps to expect. However, as noted above, the career world is changing, and there are fewer and fewer standard paths visible in occupations and organizations.

Throughout the developed world, we are seeing people struggle with entry into and progress through their careers as they confront relatively weaker job prospects and markets, less stability in employment, and ever-growing demands for advanced degrees and higher educational credentials. Structurally, high levels of unemployment still linger, thus making fewer jobs available to meet the expectations of job seekers, even the well-educated who are streaming out of colleges and universities across the globe. The rise of the so-called "accordion family" is a noticeable result as adult children, unable to get their careers underway, return home after college for indefinite and sometimes lengthy periods (Newman, 2012). Faced with the high costs of living and the scarcity of decent, entry-level jobs, the family for many university graduates serves as the shelter from the storm and the welfare state of first resort.

By viewing a large number of organizations and occupations one can analyze certain generic career stages: (1) a period of pre-career choosing of a field; (2) educational preparation for entry into that field; (3) formal education and training in the chosen field or occupation; (4) if one is fortunate, entry into the occupation or organization; (5) a period of additional learning, apprenticeship, and socialization; (6) a period of full use of one's talent, leading in some cases to some form of granting of "tenure" through being given permanent membership, a professional license, or some other form of certification; (7) a period of productive employment in one or more organizations; (8) a gradual branching into administrative, managerial, coaching, or mentoring roles and other forms of becoming a "leader"; (9) gradual disengagement, part-time work, and even going into other kinds of work; and (10) eventual retirement. These generic stages are far less predictable or certain in today's world than in the past, but their hold on our imagination as to what constitutes an external career are perhaps as strong as ever.

At any point in the external career, the person may discover that his or her internal career and career anchors are out of line with what the external career offers in terms of challenge, opportunities, and rewards. At that point, the person may switch to another career and start going through the stages over again, but usually in a more truncated form because the experience acquired in one career is often transferable to another. The engineer employed in a technical organization may discover a talent and desire for entrepreneurial ventures or for management and may decide to start a company or switch to an organization that provides more managerial opportunities. Some training in management may then be required, and the person may have to start at the bottom of a new career ladder.

Career stages in the external career within an organization or even across several organizations can be thought of as a series of movements along three different dimensions: (1) moving up in the hierarchical structure of the occupation or organization; (2) moving laterally across the various subfields of an occupation or functional groups of an organization; and (3) moving in toward the centers of influence and leadership in the occupation or organization. Depending on what the person is looking for in his or her internal career, movement along each of these

Figure 1. A Three-Dimensional Model of an Organization*

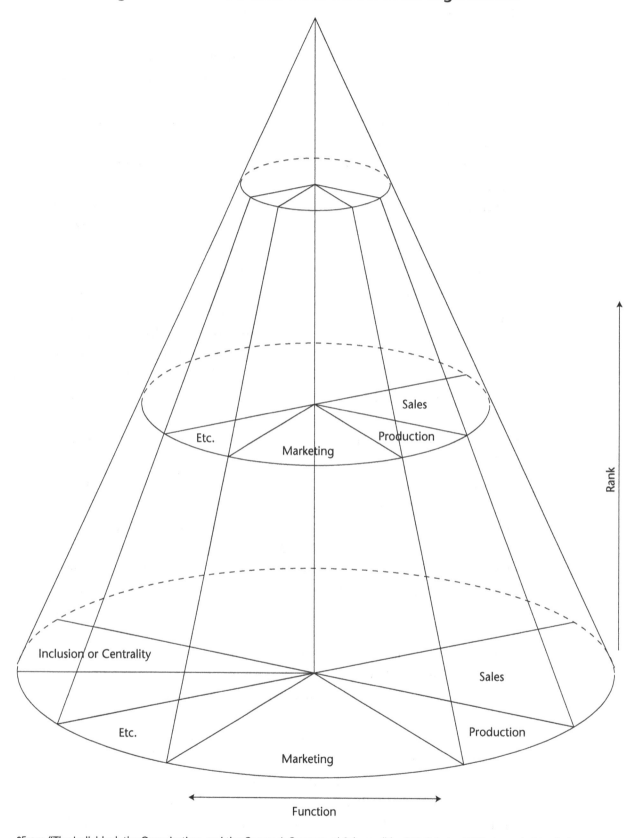

*From "The Individual, the Organization, and the Career: A Conceptual Scheme," by E.H. Schein, 1971, *Journal of Applied Behavioral Science, 7*, p. 404. Copyright 1971 by JAI Press, Inc. Reprinted by permission.

dimensions will have different meanings. For some, such as managers, it is moving up that is important; for some, such as the technical person, it is job challenge and lateral movement to new and challenging work that is most important; and for some, such as the power or socially motivated person, it is moving toward the inner circle and positions of influence that is most important. People with different career anchors will seek movement in different dimensions. Figure 1 helps to illustrate these three dimensions.

Each dimension also has its own stages associated with it, but these are usually idiosyncratic in particular occupations or organizations. In summary, career stages in the externally defined career are the sequence of roles and statuses defined by a particular occupation or organization as the way to progress through the career. They represent what we typically mark on our work resumes or use when describing to others our progress to date in the world of work and where we would like to go. Critically, they may or may not correspond to the individual's own sense of his or her internal career stages.

Development of the Career Anchor in the Internal Career

With each educational or job experience, we have an opportunity to learn. It is important to go beyond just judging each experience as good or bad, fun or not, useful or not, and to ask, "What have I learned about myself?" As we grow, we need to learn not only what is "out there" in the arena of work, but also what our own reactions are to the experiences. These reactions are best thought of in terms of three domains:

1. *Skills and competencies.* You need to learn from each experience what you are good at; that learning comes both from your own assessment and from the feedback you receive from others;

2. *Motives.* You need to learn from each experience what it is you really desire; early in life we think we know what we want, what our career aspirations are, but with each experience we discover that there are things we like or don't like, that some of our aspirations are unrealistic, and that we develop new ambitions.

3. *Values.* You need to learn from each experience what it is you value in the context of what your occupation or organization considers important, what your colleagues value, and how the kind of organizational culture you encounter fits with those values.

As you gain experience, you become more clear about each of these domains until you have a self-concept of what you are good at and not good at, want and do not want, and value or do not value. This self-concept is your *career anchor.*

The self-concept builds on whatever insight you have acquired from the experiences of youth, education, and career experience to date. However, it cannot be a mature self-concept until you have had enough real occupational experience to know what your talents, motives, and values are. Such learning may require up to ten years or more of actual work experience. If you have had many varied experiences and have received meaningful feedback with each one, your self-concept will have developed more quickly. But if you have had only a few jobs in the early years of your career and/or have obtained minimal feedback, it may take much longer.

Talents, motives, and values become intertwined so it may be hard to figure out your career anchor. People learn to be better at those things they value and are motivated to do; and they learn to value and become motivated by those things they happen to do well. They also gradually learn to avoid those things that they do not do well, although, without clear feedback, they may cling to illusions about themselves that set them up for repeated failures. Motivation without talent will eventually fade, just as talent without motivation will gradually atrophy. Conversely, new challenges can reveal latent or hidden talents and introduce a motivation that simply had not had an opportunity to appear earlier.

People differ initially as to whether it is their talents, their motives, or their values that dictate their early career choices. As time goes on, however, a need for congruence causes people to seek consistency and integration among these different elements of their self-concepts. Such a need comes about in part because others expect us to present ourselves as on a reasonably coherent career path and, in part, because we ourselves want to be on a path built on a solid foundation that moves steadily forward as we gain experience. How is this consistency learned? People first enter the world of work with many ambitions, hopes, fears, and illusions but with relatively little good information about themselves, especially about their abilities and talents. Through testing and counseling, they gain an idea of their interests, motives, and values as well as their intellectual and motor skills, but they cannot really determine how good they will be at a certain kind of work or how they will react to it emotionally.

Nowhere is this more true than in moving from a technical job into a supervisory or managerial role because of the difficulty in simulating during the educational period some of the interpersonal and emotional skills needed in those roles. Until a person actually feels the responsibility of committing large sums of money, of hiring and firing people, of saying "no" to a valued subordinate, that person cannot tell whether he or she will be able to do it or will like doing it. In many occupations, a person cannot tell whether he or she has the talent or the emotional makeup to do the job without actually performing that job.

For these reasons, the early years in an occupation are a crucial time of learning—learning about the occupation or organization and learning about oneself in relation to the demands of the job. This process is often painful and full of surprises because of the many misconceptions and illusions with which people typically enter their early work situations. Many of the dreams people have for themselves about what their work will be like may be inconsistent with their work experiences, causing "reality shock," a phenomenon that is observed in all occupations in the early years.

As you accumulate work experience, you have the opportunity to make choices; from these choices you begin to ascertain what you really find important. Dominant themes emerge—critical skills or abilities that you want to exercise or crucial needs or values that dominate your orientation toward life. You may have had a vague sense of these elements but, in the absence of actual life experience, you do not know how important they are or how any given talent, motive, or value relates in a subjective hierarchy to other elements of your total personality. Only when you are confronted with difficult choices do you begin to decide what is really important to you.

With accumulation of work experience and feedback come clarification and insight, providing a basis for making more rational and empowered career decisions. The self-concept begins to function more and more as a guidance system and as an anchor that constrains career choices. You begin to have a sense of what is "you" and what is "not you." This knowledge keeps you on course or in a safe harbor. As people recount their career choices, they increasingly refer to "being pulled back" to things they have strayed from or, looking ahead, "figuring out what they really want to do" or "finding themselves." This process leads people to gradually move from having broad goals to a sense of knowing better what it is that they would not give up if forced to make a choice. The career anchor, as defined here, is that one element in a person's self-concept that he or she will not give up, even in the face of difficult choices. And if their work does not permit expression of the anchor, people find ways of expressing it in their hobbies, in second jobs, or in leisure activities.

Identifying Career Anchors Through Career History Analysis

AN ANALYSIS OF YOUR PAST educational and occupational decisions is ultimately the most reliable way to determine your career anchor. The *Career Anchors Self-Assessment* gives you a good picture of some of the things you care about, but your past decisions and the reasons for those decisions are an even deeper basis for self-insight. You can do the history yourself by writing out your answers to the questions on pages 12 to 17, but it often works better to have a partner interview you and help you decipher your own pattern of choices.

Choose a partner with whom you are comfortable and will feel free to share the events of your career so far, as well as your future aspirations. For this reason, it is best to avoid a superior or subordinate or a peer with whom you may be in competition. Your partner does not have to be the same age you are or be in the same line of work. Ideally, your partner should be someone who knows more than a little of your past educational and work history and, therefore, will be able to help you probe and objectively analyze your educational and job history. Many people report that a spouse or a close friend makes a good partner.

Your partner does not have to have any training as an interviewer; all of the questions to be asked are provided in this booklet. All that is needed is someone who is interested and willing to discuss your career with you.

The interview should take about one hour. Give this workbook to your partner so that he or she can take notes on the interview pages before returning it to you. For each decision, try to figure out *why* you made that decision. The anchor will reveal itself gradually and will show up best in the pattern of answers to the "why's." Chances are that, even if you have moved many times, there will be a pattern to the reasons why you moved. The interview will reveal that pattern.

Career Planning Interview Questions

Education

Let's start with your education. Where did you go to high school and college? What was the reason for each choice?

What did you major in? Why?

Did you go to graduate school? Where? Why?

What was your area of concentration? Why?

First Job

What was your first real job out of school? What were you looking for in this job? Why did you make the choice you made?

What were your long-range ambitions and goals as you started your career?

How did the first job work out in terms of your goals?

What were the most important things you learned on your first job?

Next Job

When and why did you make your first job/career change? What brought this about? Why did you move?

How did this job work out in terms of your goals?

What were the most important things you learned on this job?

What was the next job change or life event? Why did it occur?

(*Interviewer:* Ask the same set of questions about each change in jobs, organizations, or life circumstances. Use additional pieces of paper if necessary.)

Review

As you look back on your career so far, do you see any major turning points? What were they and why did they occur?

What were some things you especially enjoyed in your career so far? Why?

What were some things that you did not enjoy and would like to avoid in the future? Why?

In what way have your ambitions or career goals changed? What do you now see as your long-range goals?

What is the ideal final career goal or ultimate job you would like to have?

In describing yourself to others, how do you identify your work?

What do you see to be your major competencies?

What are some critical values that guide your choice of jobs and organizations?

Do you see any pattern in your career?

The Eight Career Anchor Categories

THE EIGHT CAREER ANCHOR categories that are reviewed below were originally discovered in longitudinal research and subsequently confirmed in a variety of studies of different occupations and in different countries (Schein, 1975, 1977, 1978, 1987, 1996; Van Maanen & Schein, 1977). These were briefly reviewed in the self-assessment booklet and are explored more fully here. At the conclusion of this descriptive section, you'll have an opportunity to rate yourself from 1 to 10 on each anchor, where 1 means "This is not me at all" and 10 means "This is totally me" and check how this fits with your self-assessment scores. You can then choose a career anchor that appears to best fit you:

- Technical/Functional Competence (TF)
- General Managerial Competence (GM)
- Autonomy/Independence (AU)
- Security/Stability (SE)
- Entrepreneurial Creativity (EC)
- Service/Dedication to a Cause (SV)
- Pure Challenge (CH)
- Lifestyle (LS)

Several other categories of career concerns have been proposed over the years. However, none has shown up consistently as an "anchor"—as the one thing the person would not give up. For example, "variety," "creativity," "status or identity," and "power" have all been proposed as possible additional anchors but have not shown up consistently in research, hence are not included in the self-assessment questionnaire or in this workbook. When you examine the eight categories presented in more depth here, you will realize that every person is "concerned" to some degree with each of these issues. And most occupations make it possible to fulfill needs in several of these areas. But they are probably not equally important to you, so it is important to know their relative strength in you and, most important, what you would not give up if forced to make a choice.

To understand this concept fully and to determine your own anchor, you need to look at each of the anchors in greater detail and understand how people with different anchors diverge from one another. The following descriptions of the eight anchors are intended to provide you with this information. Each description begins with the general characteristics of the anchor and then examines the developmental issues involved, such as the type of work, pay and benefits, growth opportunities, and recognition preferred by a person with that career anchor.

Technical/Functional Competence

Some people discover as their careers unfold that they have both a strong talent and high motivation for a particular kind of work. What really "turns them on" is the exercise of their talents and the satisfaction of knowing that they are experts. This can happen in any kind of work. For example, an engineer may discover that he or she is very good at design; a salesperson may find real selling talent and desire; a manufacturing manager may encounter greater and greater pleasure in running complex plants; a financial analyst may uncover talent and enjoyment in solving complicated capital investment problems; a teacher may enjoy his or her growing expertise in the field; and so on.

We will analyze this type of person in some detail because, with the growing complexity of all business functions, it will be the technically/functionally anchored people who will supply the necessary skills for all kinds of organizations to operate. And there is every indication that the need for this kind of person will increase.

As the technically/functionally anchored people move along in their careers, they notice that if they are moved into other areas of work they are less satisfied and less skilled. They begin to feel "pulled back" to their areas of competence and enjoyment. They build a sense of identity around the content of their work, the technical or functional areas in which they are succeeding, and develop increasing skills in those areas.

The technically/functionally anchored commit themselves to a life of specialization and devalue the concerns of the general manager, although they are willing to be functional managers if it enables them to pursue their areas of expertise. Most careers start out being technical/functional in their orientation, and the early phases of many organizational careers are involved with the development of a specialty, but not everyone is excited by or uncommonly adept at a given specialty. For some people, the specialist job is a means to organizational membership or security more than it is an end in itself. For others, it is simply a stepping stone to higher rungs on the organizational ladder, a necessary step to move into general management. For still others, it is an opportunity to learn some skills or develop some connections that will be needed to launch into independent or entrepreneurial activities. Consequently, although most people start out specializing, only some find this intrinsically rewarding enough to develop career anchors around their specialties.

Preferred Type of Work

The single most important characteristic of desirable work for members of this group is that it be technically challenging to them. If the work does not test their abilities and skills, it quickly becomes boring and demeaning and will result in their seeking other assignments. Because their self-esteem hinges on exercising their talent, they need tasks that permit such exercise. Although others might be more concerned about the *context* of the work, this type of person is more concerned about the intrinsic *content* of the work.

Technical/functional people who have committed themselves to an organization (as opposed to being an autonomous consultant or craft person) are willing and anxious to share in deciding what to work on so that their efforts will be meaningful to the organization. However, once goals have been agreed on, they demand maximum autonomy in executing them. Not only do they want the autonomy in execution, but they generally also want unrestricted facilities, budgets, and resources of all kinds to enable them to perform their jobs to the best of their abilities. Conflict often emerges between general managers who are trying to limit the cost of specialized functions and the specialists who want to be able to spend whatever it takes (and the time it takes) to enable them to do the job properly as they see it.

The person anchored in this way will tolerate administrative or managerial work as long as he or she believes that it is essential to getting the job done and leads to high-quality results; however, such work is viewed as painful and necessary, rather than as intrinsically enjoyable or desirable. Being promoted into a generalist job is viewed as generally undesirable because it forces them out of the specialties with which they identify.

Talent for the interpersonal aspects of management varies in this group, resulting in the dilemma that, if such people are promoted into supervisory positions and then discover that they have no talent for supervision, they are typically blocked organizationally. Most career ladders do not provide for easy return to the technical/functional staff role once a managerial job has been taken.

Finding a viable role and challenging work as one progresses in a technical/functional career can be a difficult task, both for the individual and for the organization. Becoming more of a teacher and mentor to younger people is one workable solution. Careful redesign of work to take advantage of the experience level of the older specialist is another avenue, inasmuch as this kind of person becomes something of a generalist within his or her technical area and is thus able to bring a broader perspective to problems.

Preferred Form of Pay and Benefits

Technical/functional people want to be paid for their skill levels, usually defined by their level of education and work experience. A person with a doctorate wants a higher salary than someone with a master's degree, regardless of actual accomplishments. These people are oriented toward *external* equity, meaning that they will compare their salaries to what others of the same skill level earn in other organizations or out on their own. Even if they are the highest-paid people in their own organizations, they will feel that they are not being treated fairly if they are underpaid compared with those in similar positions in other organizations.

Technical/functional people are oriented more toward absolute pay levels than toward special incentives such as bonuses or stock options, except as forms of recognition. They probably prefer so-called "cafeteria" portable benefits, in which they choose the kinds of benefits they need (for instance, life insurance or retirement programs) because they view themselves as highly mobile and want to be able to take as much as possible with them if they decide to leave their current organizations. They are frightened of the "golden handcuffs" because they might become trapped in unchallenging work.

Preferred Growth Opportunities

Moving ahead in this group is measured by the increasing technical challenge that is provided by new job assignments. "Promotion" is also measured by increasing autonomy and support for educational opportunities. This group of people clearly prefers a professional or technical promotional ladder that functions in parallel with the typical managerial ladder. They resent promotional systems that require them to move into administration or management positions unless they are in their own area of expertise. Functional ladders have been utilized primarily in some research-and-development and engineering organizations, but they are just as applicable to all the other functional specialties that exist in organizations (such as finance, marketing, manufacturing, information technology, or sales).

Very few organizations have developed career ladders that are genuinely responsive to the growth needs of the technically/functionally anchored person. Despite the importance of this anchor to organizational growth and success—in a very real sense, the bedrock of an organization's capabilities—it is typically poorly managed, and those anchored by their technical/functional skills are among the most disenchanted among the eight anchors in their mid- to late-career stages.

Yet the technical/functional foundations of an organization rest on the hard work and expertise of those who are well educated, experienced, and attuned to high standards, for they oversee the quality of the goods or services produced and are expected to put forth innovative ideas and pass on their skills and wisdom to the next generation of specialists.

Growth for a technically/functionally anchored person does not have to be a promotion in terms of rank. If external market equity is achieved in salary, this person would respond well to being awarded an increase in the scope of the job, to being allocated more resources or areas of responsibility, to being given a bigger budget or more technical support or subordinates, or to being consulted more on high-level decisions as a result of placement on key committees or task forces.

Preferred Type of Recognition

The specialist values the recognition of his or her professional peers often more than the standard rewards—formal or informal—offered by management. In other words, a change of title or a pat on the back from a supervisor who really does not understand what was accomplished is worth less than acknowledgment from a professional peer or even from a subordinate who knows exactly what was accomplished and how difficult it might have been.

In terms of the type of recognition that is valued, at the top of the list is the opportunity for further learning and self-development in the specialty. How to remain technically sharp throughout one's career is a major concern for this group. Thus, educational opportunities, organization-sponsored sabbaticals, encouragement to attend professional meetings, budgets for buying books or equipment, and so on are highly valued. This is especially true because one of the greatest threats to technically/functionally anchored people as they age is becoming obsolete.

In addition to continuing education, this group values formal recognition through being identified to colleagues and other organization members as valued specialists. Prizes, awards, publicity, and other public acknowledgments are more important than an extra percentage in the paycheck, provided that the base pay is perceived as equitable in the first place.

Broadly viewed, the technically/functionally anchored person is most vulnerable to organizational mismanagement because organizational careers tend to be designed by general managers who value quite different things, as we will see below. The most common mistake is to take the best technical performers and make them supervisors, where they will often be either unhappy or incompetent, and sometimes both. One way to avoid such an error is to give temporary assignments to the specialist in which motivation and talent for management can be assessed both by the individual and the organization.

In terms of career movement, this kind of person wants to climb primarily a technical ladder and become more influential in his or her organization, but would and should resist either cross-functional movement or the general management ladder—especially in a multidivisional organization operating across a number of highly distinct technical domains. This is not to say, however, that those with a technical/functional anchor cannot achieve quite high positions in many organizations. Consider those finance or information technology specialists who rise to the executive committees of their respective organizations, yet at the same time resist moving into a general management role that is frequently seen by them as "too political," "too removed from their world," or "too dependent on social networking skills and who one knows rather than what one knows."

General Managerial Competence

Some people—but only some, as we will see later—discover as their careers progress that they really want to become general managers, that management per se interests them, that they have the range of competencies that are required to be a general manager, and that they have the burning ambition to rise to organizational levels at which they will be responsible for major policy decisions and their own efforts will make the difference between the success and failure of the organization.

Members of this group differ from the technical/functional people in that they view specialization as "a trap," even though they recognize the necessity to know several functional areas well and accept that one must be deeply knowledgeable in one's business or industry to function well in a general manager's job. Key values and motives for this group of people are advancement up the corporate ladder to higher and higher levels of responsibility, opportunities for leadership, contributions to the success of their organizations, and elevated incomes.

When they first enter organizations, most people have aspirations to get ahead in some general sense—to climb the proverbial corporate ladder. Many of them talk explicitly of ambitions to rise to the top, but few have a realistic picture of what is actually required in the way of talents, motives, and values to make it to the top. With experience, it becomes clearer to them that they not only need a high level of motivation to reach the top, but that they also need a mixture of talents and skills in the following three basic areas:

Analytical Competence

Analytical competence is the ability to identify, to analyze, to synthesize, and to solve problems under conditions of incomplete information and uncertainty. General managers continually point out the importance of being able to decipher what is going on; to cut through a mass of possibly irrelevant detail to get to the heart of a matter; to judge the reliability and validity of information in the absence of clear verification opportunities; and, in the end, to pose the problem or question in such a way that it can be worked on. Financial, marketing, technological, human, and other elements have to be combined into problem statements that are relevant to the future success of the organization.

It is commonly said that general managers are decision-makers. However, it is probably more accurate to say that general managers are capable of identifying, framing, and articulating problems in such a way that decisions can be made and the grounds on which such decisions rest are understood by others. General managers manage the decision-making process; to do this, they must be able to think cross-functionally, collectively, and integratively. That, in turn, requires other competencies.

Interpersonal and Intergroup Competence

This type of competence is the ability to influence, to inspire, supervise, lead, handle, and control people at all levels of the organization toward organizational goal achievement. General managers point out that this skill involves eliciting valid information from others, being able to hear and act on information coming from below, helping others to collaborate to achieve synergistic outcomes, motivating people to contribute what they know to the problem-solving process, communicating clearly the goals to be achieved, facilitating the decision-making process and decision implementation, monitoring progress, and instituting corrective action if necessary.

Much of the technical information that goes into decision making increasingly is in the hands of engaged and bright subordinates and peers with technical/functional career anchors. Therefore, the quality of decisions largely hinges on the ability of general managers to bring the right people together for problem-solving purposes and then to create norms that encourage full exchange of information and full commitment from these people. As organizations become more technically complex and global, they also become more multicultural, which means that general managers must create the conditions for cross-cultural communication and dialogue. More and more decision making occurs these days in multifunctional and multicultural groups because the complexity of the problems requires bringing together people with differing perspectives and points of view, thus necessitating the use of sophisticated group skills on the part of those in charge to get the most out of such groups. As problems become more complex, so too do the social and political difficulties of integrating the many agendas and approaches across individuals and groups into a coherent strategy and successfully implementing it.

New managers often wonder whether they will be any good at supervising others and, of almost equal importance, whether they will like supervising and managing complex group situations. Most new managers do not know what interpersonal skills they have or need unless they have been in previous leadership roles—whether in school, in the military, or in volunteer organizations. This is one reason why management recruiters are anxious to know about extracurricular activities when they assess candidates for general management jobs. Any evidence of a track record in this area is of great value, both to the individual and to the organization. Once a new manager has had an opportunity to test herself or himself—on a project team or leading a task group—and finds that the interpersonal work is manageable and enjoyable, self-confidence and ambition increase rapidly.

People who discover either that they are not talented in supervision or that they do not really like this kind of work gravitate toward other pursuits and build their career anchors around other areas, such as their technical/functional competencies, their need for autonomy, or even their interests in entrepreneurial activity. It is crucial for organizations to create career systems that make it possible for such people to move out of supervisory roles if they are not suited to or interested in such roles, preferably without penalty. All too often the best engineer or salesperson is promoted to be a supervisor, only to fail in the role, but then is stuck in it, to the inevitable detriment of his or her career and the effectiveness of the organization.

Emotional Competence

Emotional competence encompasses the capacity to be stimulated by organizational problems that create emotional and interpersonal issues and crises. Rather than be exhausted or debilitated by such challenges, it is the capacity to bear high levels of responsibility without becoming paralyzed and the ability to exercise power and make difficult decisions without guilt or shame that is the mark of the general manager.

General managers who are interviewed about their work refer to the painful process of learning to make "tough" decisions, and almost all of them say that they had not anticipated what it would be like or how they would react. Only as they gained confidence in their abilities to handle their own feelings did they gain confidence that they could really succeed as general managers. They cited as examples such decisions as laying off a valued older employee; deciding between two programs, each backed by valued subordinates; committing large sums of money to a project, knowing that the fate of many people depended on success or failure; asking a subordinate to perform a very difficult job that he or she might not want to do; inspiring a demoralized organization; fighting for a project at a higher level; delegating to subordinates and leaving them alone enough to learn how to do things; shutting down a project or a division that may leave hundreds or thousands of people out of a job; moving a plant out of a community knowing that it spells economic doom for that community; and taking ownership of a decision, in the sense of being accountable even without control over its implementation.

Most general managers report that such decisions must be made repeatedly and that one of the most difficult aspects of the job is functioning day after day, twenty-four hours a day, every day of the week, without giving up or having a nervous breakdown. It is a role that requires something of an "iron gut." It is also a role that requires a 24/7 commitment; one can never be unavailable. Indeed, the general manager is the human face of the organization and is deeply embedded, tied to, and (rightly or wrongly) held accountable for the ever-present and multifaceted problems encountered by the organization. The essence of the general manager's job is to absorb the emotional strains of uncertainty, interpersonal conflict, and responsibility. It is this aspect of the job that often repels the technically/functionally, service, or lifestyle anchored individual but excites and motivates the managerially anchored individual.

General managers differ from people with other anchors, primarily in that they have a combination of analytical competence, interpersonal and intergroup skills, and emotional competence. They cannot function well without a high degree of competence in each of these areas. It is the combination of skills that is essential for the general manager, while the technical/functional person can get along on high development of one skill element. General managers are quite different in these respects from functional managers, and it takes longer to learn to be an effective general manager because these competencies can only be learned through actual experiences.

Preferred Type of Work

People with a general management anchor want high levels of responsibility; challenging, varied, and integrative work; leadership opportunities; and chances to contribute to the success of their organizations. They will measure the attractiveness of a work assignment in terms of its importance to the success of the organization, and they will identify strongly with the organization and its success or failure as a measure of how well they have done. In a sense, then, they are real "organization people," whose identity rests on having an effective organization to manage. This sense of identity contrasts sharply with the technically/functionally anchored person, whose identity derives from the professional or technical peer group inside and outside the organization.

Preferred Form of Pay and Benefits

Managerially anchored people measure themselves by their income levels and expect to be very highly paid. In contrast to many of the other anchors, they are oriented more toward *internal* equity than external equity. They want to be paid substantially more than the level below them and will be satisfied if that condition is met, even if someone at their own level in another company is earning more. As their rank and level of accountability increases, they want the gap over subordinates to become ever greater, as illustrated by the extreme compensation of CEOs relative to others in their organizations. They also want short-term rewards, such as bonuses for achieving organizational targets, and, because they are identified with the organization, they are very responsive to things such as stock options that give them a sense of ownership and shared fate.

Managerially anchored people share with security-oriented people a willingness (if not a positive desire) for the "golden handcuffs," particularly in the form of good retirement (or "walk away") benefits such as "golden parachutes." So much of a managerially anchored person's career is tied up with a given company that his or her particular skills may not be portable in mid-life or later. However, an increasing number of general managers now shift from company to company and take their benefit packages with them or negotiate for equivalent packages. Inasmuch as intimate knowledge of a particular industry and company are important to the decision-making process, it is not clear whether such movement is or can be successful.

New specialties are arising within general management itself, such as the "turnaround manager," who is brought into a failing company from outside to bring it back to a profitable status; the "start-up manager," whose specialty is to open new parts of the organization in overseas locations or to develop new products or markets; or the "project manager," who is brought in to integrate many functions in a complex enterprise, such as developing a major weapons system or new aircraft or building an oil refinery.

Preferred Growth Opportunities

Managerially anchored people prefer promotion to a higher level or greater responsibility based on merit, measured performance, and results. Even though they acknowledge that personality, style, seniority, politics, and other factors play a role in determining promotions, general managers believe that the ability to obtain results is—and should be—the deciding criterion. All other factors are legitimate only because they are essential to getting results.

Preferred Type of Recognition

The most important forms of recognition for managerially anchored people are promotions to positions of higher responsibility. They measure such positions by a combination of rank, title, salary, number of subordinates, and size of budget, as well as by less tangible factors defined by their superiors (such as the importance of a given project or department or division to the future of the company). They expect promotions frequently. If they are too long in a given job, they assume that they are not performing adequately or are not appreciated.

Every organization's culture develops explicit or implicit timetables for promotions, and managers measure their successes partly by whether they are moving in accordance with their organizations' timetables. Thus, movement itself becomes an important form of recognition, unless it is clearly lateral or downward. Organizations sometimes develop implicit career paths that become known informally to the more ambitious general managers. It may be commonly understood, for example, that one should move from finance to marketing, then take over a staff function in an overseas company, then move to headquarters, and eventually take over a division. If promotions do not follow the typical path, these people will worry that they are "off the fast track" and are losing their potential. For this reason, movement to the "right job" is another important form of recognition.

This group of people is highly responsive to status symbols such as large offices, cars, or special privileges, and, most importantly, the approval of their superiors. Whereas the technically/functionally anchored person only values approval from someone who really understands his or her work, general managers value approval specifically from the superiors who control their most important incentive—promotion to the next-higher level.

In summary, the person who is anchored in general managerial competence and who therefore aspires to a position in general management has a very different orientation from others in the organization, even though he or she may start in a very similar kind of job. Such an orientation develops as soon as the person has acquired enough data to determine whether or not he or she has the analytical, interpersonal, and emotional skills to be a general manager. Some people have these insights early. If the organization does not respond to their needs to rise quickly, they will seek out other organizations that permit them to reach responsible levels more rapidly.

It is important to note that opportunities for realizing the general management career appear to be declining, particularly in Europe, North America, and Japan. Some of this is, of course, due to the Great Recession beginning in 2007, in which both private and public organizations have undertaken severe cutbacks in staffing levels, including the hollowing out of middle management ranks so necessary to provide the experience and learning to undertake a general management position. But this flattening trend transcends recent economic conditions and is linked to a variety of conditions, including, perhaps most importantly, globalization and increased competition. Many companies, fearful of losing markets for goods and services, have since the 1980s been steadily restructuring their labor markets and organizational designs to reduce their wage bills. Jobs that were once part of an expected career path, well-paid and more or less protected from lay-offs—including a number of middle and upper management ones—are now gone and are not likely to return.

One potentially bright spot in this picture is that certain managerial tasks have been pushed further down the organizational ranks such that the need for the general management of complex tasks, programs, or projects may well be increasing despite the disappearance of higher-level managerial roles. These may not be permanent positions—an assignment, for example, lasting only for the duration of a given project—but such roles are organizationally and perhaps developmentally critical to those who undertake them. This, along with a rather general broadening of all occupational roles as organizations become flatter and positions less narrowly defined, may modestly counter the shrinking opportunities to test and realize a general management career.

Global competition is taking us into unchartered waters, reshaping careers in ways scarcely imagined thirty or so years ago. It is now probably safe to say that there are fewer general managerial jobs available but that competition for them has grown. "Moving up," so central to the general manager's career, has become for many, if not most in this group, a lengthier process and more difficult to achieve. As Khurana (2002) shows, even at the pinnacle of the general manager career in the United States, the CEO level, there is considerably more turnover, uncertainty, and, of course, insecurity than in times past.

Autonomy/Independence

Some people discover early in their working lives that they cannot stand to be bound by other people's rules, procedures, working hours, dress codes, and other norms that almost invariably arise in any kind of organization. Regardless of what they work on, such people have an overriding need to do things in their own way, at their own pace, and according to their own standards. They find organizational life to be restrictive, irrational, and intrusive into their private lives and even their work; therefore, they prefer to pursue more independent careers on their own terms or attach themselves to only those organizational jobs that provide maximum freedom, such as being a salesman out in the field or a researcher fully in charge of her own lab. If forced to make a choice between a present job that permits autonomy and a much better job that requires giving it up, the autonomy/independence-anchored person would stay in his or her present job. Feeling free to do and say what one wants to do and say is very much valued by those with this career anchor.

Everyone has some need for autonomy, and this need varies during the course of life. For some people, however, this need comes to be overriding; they feel that they must be masters of their own ship at all times. Sometimes extreme autonomy needs result from being an only child or from high levels of education and professionalism, where the educational process itself teaches the person to be totally self-reliant and responsible, as is the case for many doctors and professors. Sometimes such feelings are developed in childhood by child-rearing methods that put great emphasis on self-reliance and independent judgment.

People who begin to organize their careers around such needs gravitate toward autonomous professions. If interested in business or management, they may go into consulting or teaching. Or they may end up in areas of work in which autonomy is relatively possible even in large organizations, such as research and development, field sales offices, legal services, market research, financial analysis, or the management of geographically remote units.

Preferred Type of Work

If autonomy-anchored persons are working in an organization, they prefer clearly delineated, time-bound kinds of work within their areas of expertise. Contract or project work, whether part-time, full-time, or even temporary, is acceptable and often desirable. Highly educated contract workers, the so-called "gold collar temps" or "gurus," are a rapidly increasing part of the American labor force and many no doubt are in such roles because they are able to dictate the terms of their employment. Specifically, they want work that comes with clearly defined goals but leaves the means of accomplishment up to them. Autonomy-anchored persons cannot stand close supervision; they might agree to organization-imposed goals or targets but want to be left alone after those goals are set to do the work in their own way.

Preferred Form of Pay and Benefits

Autonomy-anchored persons are terrified of the "golden handcuffs." They would prefer merit pay for performance, immediate payoffs, bonuses tied to short-term performance, and other forms of compensation with no strings attached. They prefer portable, cafeteria-style benefits that permit them to select the options most suitable to their life situations at given points in time.

Preferred Growth Opportunities

These persons respond most markedly to promotions that reflect past accomplishments; they would want a new job to have even more freedom than the previous one. In other words, promotion must provide more autonomy. However, being given more rank or responsibility can threaten an autonomy-anchored person if it entails a loss of autonomy. An autonomous sales representative knows that to become sales manager might mean less freedom not more, so he or she might well turn down such a promotion. A professor knows that becoming a department chair or dean means less freedom and may therefore elect to remain a professor. Typically, those with an autonomy anchor are not good team players and prefer independence to interdependence, going it alone as opposed to doing it together. As a career anchor, it appears to be a growing one (somewhat aligned in time with the growth of part-time and temporary positions in many organizations). It also is a valued anchor—or at least should be—in the sense that it ensures that some in the organization will speak openly and frankly ("truth to power") without fear of firing or ostracism if what is said is unpopular or expresses unconventional wisdom.

Preferred Type of Recognition

The autonomy-anchored person responds best to forms of recognition that are portable. Letters of commendation, testimonials, medals, prizes, awards, formal acknowledgement of an independent contribution to the organization, and other such rewards probably mean more than promotions, title changes, or even financial bonuses. Most organizational reward systems are not at all geared to dealing with the autonomy-anchored person. Hence such people often leave in disgust, complaining about organizational red tape. If their talents are not needed, no harm is done. But if key people in the organization, such as computer programmers, financial analysts, or field sales representatives, have autonomy anchors, it becomes important to redesign personnel systems to make organizational life more palatable to them.

Such redesign is often particularly difficult if the autonomy-anchored person is a permanent employee subject to all the day-to-day routines and restrictions of the organization as well as reporting to and being assessed by others in the organization and, thus, almost by definition, reducing his or her autonomy. Such individuals are certainly anti-authoritarian and, to a lesser degree, anti-authority. Sometimes creating an "individual contributor" role—as either a full- or part-time member—will be effective. But it remains the case that managing those who wish not to be managed is a most tricky matter.

Security/Stability

Some people have an overriding need to organize their careers so that they feel safe and secure, so that future events are predictable, and so that they can relax in the knowledge that they have "made it." Everyone needs some degree of security and stability throughout life, and at certain life stages financial security can become the overriding issue, such as when one is raising and educating a family, helping with the elder care of one's parents, or approaching retirement. However, for some people, security and stability are predominant throughout their careers, to the point that these concerns guide and constrain all major career decisions.

Security/stability-anchored people often seek jobs in organizations that provide some form of job tenure, that have the reputation of avoiding layoffs, that have good retirement plans and benefit programs, and that have the image of being strong and reliable. For this reason, government and civil service jobs are often attractive to these people.

Security/stability-anchored people welcome "golden handcuffs" where they are offered and are usually willing to give responsibility for their career management over to their employers. They obtain some of their satisfaction from identifying closely with their organizations, even if they do not have high-ranking or important jobs. In exchange for "tenure," they are willing to be told what work to do, how much to travel, where to live, how often to switch assignments, and so on. They fill in here, then there, becoming something of a jack-of-all-trades in the organization, always on call and willing to take on tasks others may avoid. Because of this, they are sometimes perceived by those with different career anchors as lacking ambition or may be looked on with disdain by those individuals who place a high value on personal ambition, laser-like focus, competitiveness, and achievement. This stereotype is usually quite unfair because many of these individuals have risen from humble origins into fairly high-level managerial positions and have worked quite hard and against the odds to get there. When they reach middle management in large corporations, they genuinely feel they have made it because of where they started socioeconomically. In fact, those who are the most satisfied and pleased with their careers to date are often those anchored in this domain. The highly talented among this group may indeed reach high levels in organizations while preferring (and shaping) jobs that require a steady, consistent performance. The less talented may level off in middle management or in staff jobs and gradually become less involved.

Preferred Type of Work

Security/stability-anchored people prefer predictable, enduring work and are more concerned about the context of the work than the nature of the work itself. Job enrichment, job challenge, and other intrinsic motivational tools matter less to them than improved pay, pleasant working conditions, collegial co-workers, and decent benefits. Much organizational work has this character, and every organization is highly dependent on having among its employees a large number of people anchored in security and in technical/functional competence. The overall performance of the organization is, after all, grounded on the dependable, routine, and largely—but regretfully—taken-for-granted everyday work accomplished by those committed to getting products out the door or services provided to clients and customers. Over the years, the security/stability anchored employees become keepers of the organizational culture and traditions and serve often as standard bearers for the "right and proper" way to do things in the organization—including, for example, the way employees and customers are to be treated.

Preferred Pay and Benefits

The person anchored in security/stability prefers to be paid in steadily predictable increments based on length of service. Such a person prefers benefit packages that emphasize generous insurance, medical, and retirement programs. Stock options and other forms of golden handcuffs are preferable to bonuses or other forms of unpredictable pay.

Preferred Growth Opportunities

The security/stability-anchored person prefers a seniority-based promotion system and welcomes a published grade-and-rank system that spells out what one must accomplish and how long one must serve in any given grade before promotion can be expected. Obviously, this kind of person relishes a formal tenure system such as is found in schools and universities or quasi-tenure systems associated with various forms of low-key and settled professional partnerships such a law firms.

Preferred Type of Recognition

The security/stability-anchored person wants to be recognized for his or her loyalty to the firm or organization and steady performance, preferably with reassurances of further stability and continued employment. Above all, this person needs to believe that loyalty makes a real contribution to the organization's performance and one's willingness to do "whatever it takes" to help the company succeed will be, in the end, rewarded. Most personnel systems used to be well geared to this kind of person. Today, however, guarantees of tenure are rare. A flexible labor force is the new ideal, one that can be notched up when times are good and notched down when times are bad.

Flexibility in the labor force, however, means precariousness for the individual. Moreover, loyalty is often seen now as a reflexive or knee-jerk adherence to the "old ways of doing things" and not sufficiently innovative or forward thinking to push the organization ahead. For these reasons and more, it is the security-anchored person who is typically the most vulnerable as external career systems shift away from employment security toward short-term contracts, individualized and competitive incentive plans, and reduction of head counts and redundancies.

Entrepreneurial Creativity

Some people discover early in life that they have an overriding need to create new ventures of their own by developing new products or services, by building new organizations through financial manipulation, or by taking over existing businesses and reshaping them to their own specifications. Creativity in some form or other exists in all of the career anchor groups, but what distinguishes the entrepreneur is that creating a new venture of some sort is viewed as the *essence* of the career itself and is therefore vital to self-fulfillment. Inventors or artists or researchers also depend heavily on creativity, but they usually are not committed to building new ventures around their creations. The creative urge in the entrepreneurial anchor group is specifically aimed toward creating new organizations, products, or services that can be identified closely with the entrepreneur's own efforts, that will survive on their own, and that will be economically successful. Making money then becomes one key measure of success.

Many people dream about forming their own businesses and express those dreams at various stages of their careers. In some cases, these dreams express needs for autonomy—to get out on one's own, beyond the control of others. However, entrepreneurially anchored people typically pursue such dreams relentlessly and begin relatively early in life, often having started small money-making enterprises even during high school. They found out early that they had both the talent and an extraordinarily high level of motivation to prove to the world that they could do it.

It is important to distinguish this career anchor from the autonomy/independence one. Many people want to run their own businesses because of autonomy needs and may fulfill those needs by buying small businesses, which they then can run independently. What distinguishes entrepreneurs is their obsession with proving that they can *create* businesses. And they usually discover rather quickly that autonomy is hardly the name of the game, since they are in many ways closely monitored and restricted by those who fund their ventures, by partners and employees with whom they must agreeably work, by time pressures and the need to generate return on investments, by demanding customers or clients, and a bundle of other constraints.

Entrepreneurial creation often therefore means sacrificing both autonomy and stability, particularly in the early stages before a business is successful. Entrepreneurially anchored people often fail in their efforts but keep searching for opportunities to try again and again. They may hold conventional jobs while planning their next efforts and even build their enterprises "on the side." For example, a person may be a sales representative or a middle manager in some organization while trying to build a real-estate empire or looking for a company to acquire and run in his or her spare time. What makes such a person an "entrepreneur" is the dedication to creating the new enterprise and the willingness to drop a pre-existing job once a venture has been located and launched.

It is worth pointing out that most entrepreneurial attempts fail. Persistence, good luck, and being in the right place at the right time surely all play a role, as does having an innovative and creative idea and the organizational abilities to bring it to fruition. If those anchored by security/stability concerns are the most satisfied among the eight anchor groups, those anchored by entrepreneurial creativity are the least satisfied on average. The reasons include the high failure rates associated with entrepreneurial ventures but also the fact that, even if a venture succeeds, it is not the running of an ongoing organization that drives the entrepreneur but rather the creative act of bringing it into existence in the first place. Directing an ongoing concern is typically unexciting and mundane to the entrepreneur, who looks quickly to move on and start something new again. Hence a constant restlessness is associated with this anchor and, in this sense, the entrepreneur is never truly satisfied since there is always another start-up opportunity just around the corner.

Preferred Type of Work

Entrepreneurially anchored people are obsessed with the need to create and they tend to bore easily. In their own enterprises, they may continue to invent new products or services, or they may lose interest, leave these enterprises, and begin afresh. They are restless and continually require new creative challenges. If they are employed in organizations while they are planning their own ventures, they require jobs that either give them enough autonomy to pursue their side ventures or train them for the future, such as would be the case of the engineer who learns enough about a given product in an employing organization to eventually go out on his own with some new version of that product.

Preferred Pay and Benefits

For this group of people, ownership is ultimately the most important issue. Often they do not pay themselves very well, but they retain control of their organizations' stock. If they develop new products, they want to own the patents. Large organizations that attempt to retain entrepreneurs often misunderstand the intensity of these needs. Unless given control of the new enterprise with patents and 51 percent of the stock, an entrepreneurially anchored person will not stay with an organization, even though it offers to invest in his or her enterprise. Entrepreneurs want to accumulate wealth, not so much for its own sake but as a way of showing the world what they have accomplished. Benefit packages are not a central issue to them.

Preferred Growth Opportunities

Entrepreneurs want career systems that permit them to be wherever they need to be at any given point during their careers. Most of them want to be the heads of their organizations, but often the managerial duties that are involved do not fit their talents or desires. In particular, if their ventures are to be successful in the long haul, it often requires good general management, something that the entrepreneur might not be good at and might not like to do. They then want the power and the freedom to move into other roles they consider to be key to the venture and to meet their own needs, usually roles that permit them to continue to exercise creativity, such as head of research and development, chairman of the board, or in charge of all new investments. In many cases, if these roles prove tiresome, they sell their organizations and start new ones to fulfill their creative needs.

Preferred Type of Recognition

Building fortunes and sizeable enterprises are two of the most important ways that members of this group achieve recognition. In addition, entrepreneurs are rather self-centered, seeking high personal visibility and public recognition. "Whose name is on the building" (or product, organization, etc.) is often a major concern. For some, called "serial entrepreneurs," the need to create plays out by starting companies, selling them, and starting new ones. The more successful ventures this kind of entrepreneur has across a career, the more successful the career. The energy required to follow such careers is enormous and may well wax and wane. In many ways, however, this is a young person's game since the ceaseless looking about and chasing down entrepreneurial opportunities that often do not pan out surely takes a personal toll on the entrepreneur, which is likely to increase over time.

Sense of Service/Dedication to a Cause

Some people enter occupations because of central values that they want to express in their work and careers. They are oriented more toward these values than toward their actual talents or the areas of competence involved. Their career decisions are based on the desire to improve the world in some fashion. People with this anchor are attracted to the helping professions such as medicine, nursing, research, social work, teaching, and the ministry and to the many nonprofit organizations or NGOs. However, dedication to a cause clearly also characterizes some people in business management and in their organizational careers. Some examples include the human resource specialist who works on affirmative action programs, the labor lawyer intent on achieving social justice or improving labor-management relations, the biotech research scientist working on a new drug, the scientist working for environmental protection, the engineer working to enhance manufacturing sustainability, or the manager who chooses to go into public service in order to improve some aspect of society in general.

Values such as working for and with people, serving humanity, saving the environment, and helping one's nation can be powerful anchors for one's career. The defining feature of such careers involves working for a "higher cause" more so than working for an organization. Such higher causes can, of course, vary and vary spectacularly. It is an activist role that animates the career, but one might advocate for or against the primacy of shareholder values, for or against policies that seek to limit climate change, for or against equal opportunity initiatives in the workplace. What is central, however, is the crusading element of the career and the commitment to goals that the person genuinely believes will benefit the larger society.

It is important to note, however, that the so-called helping or service professions are also attractive to the other anchor groups discussed so far. One can be a technically expert or managerially anchored social worker or lawyer; one can pursue a career in medicine or teaching for autonomy or security reasons. Each of these occupations affords opportunities for entrepreneurship and general management. In other words, one should not assume that all people in service-type jobs have service anchors.

Preferred Type of Work

Service-anchored people clearly want work that permits them to influence their employing organizations in the direction of their values. In this sense they are "moral entrepreneurs" seeking to influence and persuade others. A good example of this kind of person is a professor of agriculture who left a tenured university position to accept a job as manager of environmental planning for a large mining company. He stated that he would continue to work for this company as long as he was allowed to do key environmental planning and to have the power to accomplish things.

Preferred Pay and Benefits

People anchored in sense of service, a "calling" or dedication to a cause, want level playing fields, fair pay for their contributions, and portable benefits because they have no a priori organizational loyalty. Money per se is not central to them but, like the technical/functional people, they are concerned about external equity, that is, being paid fairly in relation to what others in their fields receive.

Preferred Growth Opportunities

For this group, more important than monetary rewards is a promotional system that recognizes their contributions and moves them into positions with more and more influence and the freedom to operate more autonomously. They want their causes to be heard and acted on by others in the organization. Rotational systems that move such persons into higher-ranking areas where their values become either irrelevant or marginal to the work they take on are clearly undesirable, but professional ladders that provide higher rank and influence within their service-oriented fields are desirable.

Preferred Type of Recognition

Service-anchored people want recognition and support, both from their professional peers and from their superiors; they want to feel that their values are well understood and shared by higher levels of management. Like the technically/functionally anchored, they appreciate opportunities for more education, support for attendance at professional meetings, awards and prizes, and public acclaim for their accomplishments.

Pure Challenge

Some people's careers are driven by a need to prove over and over again that they can conquer anything or anybody. There are engineers, for example, who only are really motivated when someone tells them that "no one has been able to solve this problem before." They define success as overcoming impossible obstacles, solving unsolvable problems, or winning out over extremely tough opponents. As they progress, they seek ever-tougher challenges. For some, this takes the form of seeking jobs in which they face more and more difficult problems. However, these people are not technically/functionally anchored because they seem not to care in what area the problem occurs.

Some high-level strategy/management consultants seem to fit this pattern in that they relish more and more difficult kinds of strategic assignments, no matter what the industry or the company. Private equity traders on Wall Street seem to thrive on pure challenge, measuring their success by closing bigger and bigger deals and forever besting the competition (Ho, 2009). Project leaders for oil and gas exploration seem to take delight in arduous assignments that take them to the world's most remote, inaccessible, and dangerous locations. The harder the job, the more it is welcome. Repetitive tasks, no matter how complicated or difficult at the outset, are of little interest. Increasing difficulty matters to those anchored by pure challenge, and the cliché "been there, done that" symbolizes tasks best avoided.

For some, the challenge is defined in interpersonal and competitive terms. For example, some naval aviators perceive their sole purpose in life is to prepare themselves for the ultimate confrontation with an enemy (Derr, 1986). In that confrontation, these "warriors" would prove to themselves and to the world their superiority in competitive combat. Although the military version of this anchor may seem somewhat over-dramatized, people in many other occupations also define life in such competitive terms. Many salespeople, professional athletes, scientific researchers, software developers, and even some general managers and entrepreneurs define their careers essentially as daily combat or competition in which *winning* is everything.

Most people seek a certain level of challenge, but for the person anchored in pure challenge, it is the one thing that matters most. The area of work, the kind of employing organization, the pay system, the type of promotion system, and the forms of recognition are all subordinate to whether or not the job provides constant opportunities for self-tests. In the absence of such constant tests of self, the person becomes bored and irritable. Often such people talk about the importance of variety in their careers, and one reason some of them are attracted to general management is the variety and intense challenge that managerial situations can provide.

People anchored in pure challenge can also be very single-minded, combative, and can certainly make life difficult for those who do not have comparable aspirations. The 1979 Hollywood film *The Great Santini* depicted the problems created by a "warrior," both for his supervisors and for his family because there were no wars to be fought. A career for such a person has meaning only if competitive skills can be exercised; if there is no such opportunity, the person can become demoralized and hence a problem to him- or herself and others.

Preferred Types of Work, Pay, Benefits, and Recognition

The types of work desired, pay and benefits, career growth, and forms of recognition will vary immensely in this group as a function of the actual kind of "pushing the envelope" work they are doing. Some may wish for an individually customized pay-for-performance plan; others may opt for guaranteed rewards allowing them to risk failure. Still others may feel most challenged by a winner-take-all form of compensation. Across the board, those anchored by pure challenge typically see the world in almost Darwinian terms, a dog-eat-dog world where only the fit and strong survive. But, given the wide range of occupations and organizations in which the anchor is found, no easy generalizations as to the type of work, pay, benefits, and forms of recognition can be put forth. We need only compare the variation in these factors among "warriors," professional athletes, bond salesmen, turn-around managers, game developers, some scientists, and engineers working on unsolved problems to see that there are no easy generalizations for this group, as is also the case for the next group.

Lifestyle

At first glance, this concept seems like a contradiction in terms. People who organize their existence around lifestyle are, in one sense, saying that their work careers are less important to them than other aspects of their lives and, therefore, that they do not really have a career anchor. These people do belong in a discussion of career anchors, however, because a growing number of people who are highly motivated toward meaningful work careers are, at the same time, finding themselves in situations in which their careers must be integrated with their personal needs, family situations, and, when relevant, their partners' careers.

This situation has arisen for more and more people because of (1) changing social values around independence, (2) the growing number of women in full-time careers, which has led to many more dual-career families, (3) employers providing less job security and fewer, if more portable, benefits, and (4) the growing number of families who cannot survive economically unless both partners work. If people are told to manage their own careers and yet they live with partners who also have careers, it is inevitable that more and more people would think about designing or redesigning their total life situations, not just their work careers (Bailyn, 2002, 2006).

Family demographics have been shifting rather noticeably over the past twenty or so years. Contemporary family structures vary considerably. A rough guide of households would include (1) single, no children; (2) single, with children; (3) DINK ("dual income, no kids"); (4) sandwich (single or dual income but supporting both parents and children); (5) married with children (dual income); (6) married with children (one earner); (7) married, no children (one earner or two), (8) single with partner (one earner or two); and so on. Of the structures listed above, the "new normal" and largest in terms of a percentage of the U.S. population as of 2010 is the solo category, living alone (Klinenberg, 2012). The fastest growing since the 1980s are the dual income categories. The old and rather idealized or demonized pattern—akin to the "Mad Men" television portrayal of the advertising work world in New York City during the 1950s and early 1960s—of having an unpaid yet supportive partner at home to attend to family duties while the other partner is fully engaged in a paid work career now characterizes only a small minority (around 10 to 12 percent) of U.S. families and is continuing to fall (U.S. Census Bureau, 2010). This older pattern, however, still promises higher incomes for the one earner of a family—be it male or female—than in dual career families where both earners pay something of a small penalty that is apparently a result of the complications of having to coordinate two careers and hence having less time to devote solely to their respective individual work careers (Percheski, 2008; Reitman & Schneer, 2003).

What is clear, however, is that lifestyle as a career anchor varies widely across these family classifications, as does the kind of lifestyles people want and hope to realize.

Balancing personal and professional lives has always been an issue and has never been easy. In a single-career family, the common resolution was—and continues to be—that one partner's career dominates and the other performs a supportive role.

If two full careers are involved, as is increasingly the case, the balancing process is obviously much more complex, requiring economic, geographic, and other lifestyle decisions, such as whether or not or when to have children. Achieving a balance is even more difficult today because fewer jobs are "standard" in the sense that sound performance is exchanged for more or less guaranteed full-time work accompanied by fair pay and benefits.

Flexibility has become the employer's mantra, requiring even more flexibility on the part of those trying to meet the demands of the ever-changing workplace. Thirty-five percent of the U.S. labor force now works under "non-standard" conditions with few guarantees, and the largest private employer in the world today is the Milwaukee-based global temp agency Manpower that, as of 2009, counted almost five million "employees" under its placement umbrella. Significantly, 50 percent of Manpower's growth in the United States since 2000 has come from placing highly skilled professionals into temporary jobs. These jobs run the gamut from low-status ("rubbish contracts") to high ("diamond contracts") but, Manpower aside, the range, if not the numbers, of temporary or part-time managerial positions now available has grown.

Preferred Type of Work, Pay, Benefits, and Recognition

Some of these changes in the external careers available to people have undoubtedly aided those with lifestyle anchors. An integration of career and lifestyle issues is itself an evolving process, and how it is accomplished in various life stages (single, married, parent to young children, parent of college-aged children, empty-nester, grandparent) depends both on choices being available as well as a felt freedom to choose among them. Hence, people with a lifestyle anchor want flexibility more than anything else. Unlike the autonomy-anchored, who also want flexibility, those with lifestyle anchors are quite willing to work for organizations, do a variety of kinds of work, and accept organizational rules and restrictions, provided that the right options to step away from the workplace are available to them at the right time. Such options might include less travel or moving only at times when their family situations permit, part-time work if life concerns require it, sabbaticals, paternity and maternity leaves, day-care options (which are becoming especially relevant for the growing population of dual-career couples and single parents), flexible working hours or, for some, regular, predictable working hours (no overtime requests), the opportunity to work at home during normal working hours, and so on. American workplaces are increasingly being rated in terms of just how "family friendly" or "employee centered" they are, and those anchored in lifestyle are typically intensely interested in such ratings.

Lifestyle-anchored people look more for an organizational attitude than specific programs or a set of benefits. They look for an attitude that reflects respect for the individual's personal and family concerns and an organization that makes genuine negotiation (and renegotiation) of the work contract possible. People with this anchor require understanding and flexibility from their organizations and formal personnel policies that acknowledge the reality of the lifestyle issues facing employees. At any given time, it is not clear what particular organizational responses will be most helpful, except that policies and career systems in general must become more flexible and provide choices.

One specific lifestyle issue is the growing unwillingness of career occupants to move geographically, a step that is often associated with promotion. In the past, this seemed to be an aspect of the security/stability anchor, but it has become increasingly clear that people who are unwilling to move feel this way less for security/stability reasons than for reasons of wanting to integrate personal, family, and career issues. Moving two careers or moving kids out of a desired school at a critical age is something that many people are less and less willing to do, even if it costs them a promotion or some other desired career outcome. Also, moving from a relatively low-cost-of-living area of the country to a much higher one may well threaten lifestyle-anchored people, since their quality of life—as they define it—is likely to diminish.

This trend, if it continues, could have major implications for external career paths. Many companies take it for granted that people will move when asked to do so and treat this as a positive developmental career step. If they encounter more and more people anchored in lifestyle, it is not clear whether these people will have to sacrifice career advancement or whether their companies will have to redefine career paths to make advancement more feasible within a confined geographical area.

For example, the president of a large multinational company learned recently that one of his most likely successors did not want to leave a particular geographic area because of his wife's career and their mutual desire to keep their children in a given school. The president knew that this person needed international experience to continue his career growth and tried to make it clear that if the person did not take the international assignment he would be off the promotional ladder for CEO. The person then had to choose, which meant, in essence, deciding whether his anchor was general management or, in fact, lifestyle.

Another struggle around lifestyle issues appears frequently for the person who is single, without children, and often looked to by his or her employer as the go-to person who can fill in for fellow co-workers who have family conflicts. For a manager in this position with or without a lifestyle anchor, difficulties ensue. An (in)famous case made the national news several years ago when the then-Governor of

Pennsylvania, Ed Rendell, voiced his support for Janet Napolitano's appointment as the head of Homeland Security in the following way: "Janet's perfect for that job because, for that job, you have to have no life. She has no family. This is perfect. . . perfect because she can devote nineteen or twenty hours a day to it" (*New York Times*, December 1, 2008). Those who are anchored by lifestyle clearly must build their careers on contested terrain in many organizations. For those who are married with children, sociologist Arlie Hochschild (1997) concluded her close study of such families by warning that "the corporation's fiercest struggle has been with its local rival—the family."

In sum, managing to successfully integrate work and family concerns and/or to live a rich personal life while holding to a managerial career is perhaps the most vexing of endeavors, thus making lifestyle the most problematic of the eight anchors. If you find yourself in a situation in which the lifestyle anchor most nearly fits you, you need to figure out what kinds of compromises you are unwilling to make and what kinds you are (e.g., with your employer, your immediate boss, others close to you or in your family, your co-workers, etc.). Being clear and communicating your values and reasons for lifestyle choices are critical.

Review of Ratings and Questionnaire Scores

LOOKING BACK TO THE patterns revealed in your career history interview and having read the more detailed anchor category descriptions in the previous section, record two scores for each anchor below. In Column 1, for each anchor, rate yourself on a 10-point scale, where 1 means "this anchor does not fit me at all" and 10 means "this anchor is totally me." In Column 2, copy your total score for each anchor from the self-assessment questionnaire. The two evaluations use different scales, so *there should NOT be a numerical match*, but if you have given honest answers on the questionnaire, there should be a reasonable match in terms of the RELATIVE RANK of each anchor between your self-assessment scores and your job history ratings.

	Column 1 Job History Rating	Column 2 Self-Assessment Score
Technical/Functional Competence (TF)	_____	_____
General Managerial Competence (GM)	_____	_____
Autonomy/Independence (AU)	_____	_____
Security/Stability (SE)	_____	_____
Entrepreneurial Creativity (EC)	_____	_____
Service/Dedication to a Cause (SV)	_____	_____
Pure Challenge (CH)	_____	_____
Lifestyle (LS)	_____	_____

At this diagnostic point, it is most useful to look at your lowest ratings and scores first to see what kinds of things you do not care about. Do you agree that these are unimportant areas for you? If not, go back and review some of the items that you gave low numbers to on the self-assessment and ask yourself why you rated them the way you did. Then, look again at your career history responses to reconsider just why you gave certain anchors low ratings.

Now look at the categories that produced the highest scores. If forced to make a choice, can you identify the one thing you would not give up? Many people find at this point that there are two or three anchor categories that are high. This is normal because neither the history interview nor the self-assessment questionnaire forced you to make choices between categories. Again, the first step to further clarification is to look back at the items on the self-assessment to see whether you would still score them the same way and then to review those critical periods uncovered by your career history reconstruction to see whether your recall is complete and your anchor ratings accurately reflect this.

Many people find that they still have two or three categories that seem equally important. That means you have not had to face a situation in which one or the other had to be given up. Try to imagine such situations and see what it is that you would NOT GIVE UP. For example, a common conflict is between the technical/functional anchor and the general management anchor. Ask yourself, as you look ahead in your career, whether you would rather be the chief technologist (or the most senior person in your functional specialty) or the executive vice president (or CEO). When the choice is put this way, most people have a clear sense of which they would prefer, which tells them their real anchors.

Common Questions

AS YOU HAVE GONE THROUGH THIS ANALYSIS, several other questions will have arisen in your mind. Some of the most common are reviewed below.

Are There Other Career Anchors?

People often ask whether there are other anchors, especially ones centered around power, variety, pure creativity, or organizational identity. According to the research guideline used, if two or more cases absolutely did not fit the existing eight categories and clearly resembled each other in some dimension, an additional anchor category would be created. Thus far, each proposed dimension has proven to be an aspect of another anchor or has been expressed differently in different anchor groups.

Power and creativity, for example, seem to be universal needs that are expressed in different ways by different anchor groups. The technical/functional person expresses power through superior knowledge and skill; the entrepreneur through building and controlling an organization; the general manager through obtaining a position that provides rank, influence, resources, and decision rights; the service-oriented person through moral persuasion; and so on. Similarly, creativity can be displayed in each of the anchor categories in different ways. Variety is something else that many people want and thrive on, but it is not an anchor per se because it can be obtained through autonomy, managerial challenges, entrepreneurial activity, or lifestyle. Only those anchored in technical/functional competence, security, and service trade some aspects of variety for other important considerations in their career evolutions.

From the point of view of this exercise in self-analysis, you should attempt to locate your "true" anchor from among the eight. The future may well reveal something new about yourself and require a reassessment of your anchor but, for awareness, clarity, and diagnostic acuity, it is most useful to identify a "best fit" anchor. You should, of course, allow for the possibility that your pattern of competencies, motives, and values is unique. No one has the exact same interests, family background, personal history, or personality. What is important here, however, is to gain insight into yourself so that you make better career choices now and in the future. Locating yourself among the eight anchor categories should help you in this, but it is not necessary to force yourself to fit into one of them. What you must find out about yourself is *what you would not give up if forced to make a choice.* That is your true career anchor.

Does the Career Anchor Concept Travel?

Research to date indicates that the eight anchors presented here and applied to managerial careers turn up in a variety of occupations and appear to apply equally well to doctors, lawyers, teachers, naval officers, consultants, software developers, and even production workers—although one should expect the distributions across the anchors to vary considerably from occupation to occupation (Schein, 1987; Van Maanen & Schein, 1977). Even "nonpaying" work roles such as childcare, volunteer work, and service to one's religion can be seen in terms of the different anchors. And partners of career-involved people find that they enjoy running households for reasons that often mirror the anchor categories.

To illustrate the broader applicability of the career anchor concept, consider big city police organizations. When the careers of police officers are examined, some orient themselves toward jobs with a general management anchor, seeking advancement up the ranks. Patrol officers with this ambition might well be attending college during off-duty hours, studying conscientiously for various civil service exams, and actively searching out ways to increase their opportunities to move up in the organization. These are also officers most likely to regard everyday patrol duties as unimportant and to withdraw from them as early as (and whenever) possible. To fellow patrol colleagues, those who aspire to ranking positions in the police service—a long, problematic, and difficult climb up a steep and very narrow career ladder—are typically seen as "pencil pushers" and "brown nosers."

There are technical/functional types as well. A "cop's cop" is a tag fellow officers reserve for those who want nothing more than to cultivate and exercise their perceived police competences. Whether detectives or uniformed patrol officers, these officers regard "crook catching" as their *raison d'etre* and promotion holds little fascination for them. Indeed, rising in the ranks is viewed with some disdain, for it takes one away from the action on the streets: "We're cops, not desk-jockeys or social workers." They are likely to be fascinated by some of the technology of police work and become very adept at using it.

Security is also an identifiable anchor. Those who fall in this category—sometimes called "uniform carriers" by contemptuous colleagues—will do whatever is required to stay out of trouble and maintain their jobs. They often seek out organizational segments where stability, safety, and routine characterize their everyday tasks—communications, jail, records, quiet beats, and so on. Akin to those anchored by security are those officers who value the lifestyle a police career allows and look for those positions that do not require overtime or revolving shift work and pursue those prized personal and family interests off the job that a steady income allows. Both lifestyle and security anchors emphasize the relatively generous retirement benefits of a police career and carry what other officers regard as a "backward calendar" for, when asked about how long they have been cops, they often reply by saying, "I've only got six more years before I pull the pin and retire." Retirement may come in their early forties, thus opening up new career—or leisure—opportunities.

Entrepreneurial creativity as a career anchor can be seen in the police world as well. While rare, there are those officers who actively seek to build a successful business on the side such that they can eventually leave the police organization. Security consultancies run by ex-police officers (from all ranks) represent one example of such ventures. Less noble are those "bent" police officers who take advantage of situational opportunities to proactively build criminal businesses as heads of extortion or drug rings. Service anchors turn up in police departments too as some officers—although few in number and regarded by many of their colleagues as odd ducks and "do-gooders"—define their roles in social work terms of aiding the down-and-out and defenseless in society.

Autonomy anchors are also discoverable among, for instance, those patrol officers who prefer "solo beats" or those detectives who prefer to work their own cases without departmental or collegial interference (and are typically viewed by their managers as troublesome if not "rogue cops"). Finally, there are those police officers viewed by others (and themselves) as "gung ho" sorts who look continually for work challenges that are both dangerous and difficult. Such officers show up on SWAT teams, bomb squads, counter-terrorist units, undercover narcotics squads, and patrol units assigned to high-crime areas.

As this police example suggests, virtually any organization of sufficient size and differentiation will have most if not all of the eight career anchors represented across the employee population. Again, distributions will vary by the aims and culture of the organization. Nonprofits may find higher percentages of those with a service anchor on their payrolls; investment banks may disproportionally employ those with pure challenge and technical/functional anchors; and global automobile manufacturing firms may encourage those with general managerial anchors to join and remain with the company. But, rest assured, those with other anchors can find a place in these organizations as well.

There is, however, a good deal of interaction between the types of work, pay and benefits, growth opportunities, and types of recognition offered by organizations and the distribution of career anchors found within them. Some anchors will no doubt be better served in certain industries and organizations than in others. An information system specialist with a technical/functional anchor is probably a better fit in a high-tech manufacturing organization where collegial appreciation for the somewhat esoteric competencies of the specialist are likely to be more developed and the need for specialized work more acute than in a low-tech marketing company. And timing matters, too. In periods of retrenchment and restructuring, those with general management anchors may well find their desired paths blocked and those with technical/functional anchors may be given pink slips if their particular area of expertise is no longer viewed by senior management as critical to the business. Trying to determine just where one's career anchor will be best served both now and going forward is then an ongoing and always uncertain matter.

Can a Person Have More Than One Anchor?

A career anchor is defined as the one thing a person would not give up if forced to make a choice. This definition allows for only one anchor—the one set of talents, values, and motives at the top of one's personal hierarchy. However, many career situations make it possible to fulfill several sets of talents, motives, and values, making a choice unnecessary and thus preventing a person from finding out what is really at the top of his or her hierarchy. For example, a functional manager in a paternalistic company simultaneously can fulfill security, autonomy, technical/functional, managerial, and even lifestyle anchors. As we pointed out before, in order to determine a single anchor, that person must then invent hypothetical career options that would force a choice. For example, would that person choose to be a division general manager or the chief corporate officer in his or her function? Most people can identify their true anchors if they pose such choices to themselves.

If we are lucky, we might not have to make such a critical choice and can manage over the course of a long career a bundle of anchors without giving one or more up. There are, however, some real limits here. The first is sociological since the structure of our careers, as defined by external demands, weighs heavily on us and typically requires choices to be made if we are not to drift too far from the anchors that most define us. The second is psychological and reflects the fact that the distinctly different skills, motives, and values represented by each anchor are to varying degrees in conflict.

There are complementary elements across anchors, of course, and some anchors are more easily linked than others. But when choices must be made, the anchors lead in different directions. Thus, having your career priorities well established and thought through can help guide critical career decision making if and when the time arrives. For example, a general management anchor might complement a lifestyle anchor for a time by allowing you to afford and enjoy a way of living off the job by spending, say, a lot of time with your spouse and children or extended family and friends, residing in a handsome home in a personally beloved part of the country, playing serious tennis, running marathons, or traveling afar and extensively as an eco-tourist. But it is unlikely you could reach the pinnacle of the general manager career without sacrificing some, perhaps many, of these non-work interests and passions, whatever your income. Such sacrifices may arise gradually or may come suddenly, but having a solid understanding of your anchor priorities will enable you to make better career choices.

Sorting out and prioritizing career anchors is especially difficult for those just beginning their work careers. Without extensive work experience, it is altogether possible that certain aspects of all eight anchors seem desirable. Recent college graduates, for example, often say they want a career that offers them considerable autonomy, high levels of responsibility, the opportunity to use their technical skills, solid promotional prospects, good pay, generous benefits, lots of free time away from work, and a fair amount of job stability such that they feel secure. In other words, they want it all. But ask them five or ten years later what they want from their careers and one receives much more specific and concrete answers that might be expressed as wanting to "do deals" or "launch new products" or "found a start-up company" or "not have to relocate again" or "manage real estate portfolios" or "head up a division in the firm." Confidence in the identification of your career anchor then stems largely from the experience you have had to date (and the career choices—both good and bad—you have made in the past) and what you learned from such experiences.

If no anchor emerges clearly for you, it is likely that you have not had enough life experience to develop priorities that determine how to make career choices. In this situation, you might benefit from determining what anchors seem the most important to you and then explore your reactions to different situations through systematic job choices as your career advances. For example, if you do not know whether you have a talent or taste for general management and have had no opportunities to work in this area, you might volunteer to run a project, become a committee chairperson, ask to be acting manager of a unit, or try to gain experience in some other way. In lieu of this, you might find people who are clearly in the kind of job situations where you think you might have both an aptitude and interest and interview them in detail about what it is like to be in those positions.

Do Anchors Change?

All the evidence is not in yet as to whether or not anchors change. Too few people have been studied for long enough periods of time to determine how career anchors evolve. However, many of the original panelists in this research from the 1960s were followed into their mid-forties and fifties. Thus far, the weight of evidence is on the side of stability. One would expect this because, as people clarify their self-images—as they become more aware of what they are good at, want, and value—they tend to want to hold onto those self-images. And the better people know themselves, the more they want to hold onto that hard-won insight.

Examples are useful here. Consider first a technically/functionally anchored engineering manager in a large corporation who found himself moving toward general management because of the nature of the external career path. Because he sensed that his next promotion would be to a generalist job, he began to lobby among his friends in senior management to be assigned to a high-level staff job at headquarters, and he successfully created this lateral move. He was willing to give up a promotion to a higher-level general management job to remain in his preferred technical area. Another technical/functional manager resigned because the job was boring to her and she was "dead-ended." She then picked up her career as a successful consultant in that same technical/functional area. Her career changed, but her anchor did not. Finally, consider the autonomy-anchored salesman who dropped out of organizational life altogether and lived a marginal life until he married and had children. Instead of returning to the mainstream, he and his wife opened an antique shop that permitted him to remain autonomous.

Some people who make dramatic mid-life changes in their external careers are trying to actualize what were their anchors all along; they simply never had the chance to do what they really wanted to do. One example is a corporate financial analyst with a service anchor who, having served what she called "a too lengthy apprenticeship" in a private-sector investment bank (some fifteen years), quit the bank and used the money she had saved to join with friends who were starting a nonprofit educational venture for children with disabilities. Another example concerns a computer consultant with a technical/functional anchor who had always wanted to go to law school and finally did so when a small inheritance enabled him to finance it. Following graduation, he drifted into small-town law and developed a successful practice using many of the computer and consulting skills he had acquired. He remained anchored in the technical/functional area.

Because of the way that careers are structured, one's job and one's career anchor often do not match. A technically/functionally anchored person might be promoted to general manager, or a managerially anchored person might be given a high-level staff job. A security-anchored person might be convinced to join an entrepreneurial venture, or an autonomy-oriented person might take a boring but stable job under a controlling boss to earn money. People are able to perform in these situations and sometimes perform well, but they are not happy and do not feel that their real selves are engaged. They can adapt to circumstances and make the best of them, but their anchors do not change; as soon as there is an opportunity, they will seek a better match.

■ ■ ■

You now should have a fairly clear idea of your career anchor. If you have experienced change in your own career, ask yourself whether the anchor changed or only the concerns that were occupying you at different career and life stages changed. The next portion of this booklet is designed to look outward toward the work and family context within which you operate to help you decide whether your career anchor, present work role, and current life situation are a good match—and, if not, how you might think about areas for personal development.

Moving Ahead: Reconciling Your Anchor with the Demands of Work, Family, and Self

THE PRIMARY FOCUS UP to now has been on your own career history and the insights you have had about your competencies, your career motives, and the values that you hold strongly. The concept of career anchors captures these insights. But what are you to do next in a world in which more and more you are expected to take charge of your own career? To make intelligent plans, you need a way to analyze your present and future job, family and personal situation, a process to enable you to make decisions—among many—regarding your career: Do you want to stay where you are in your organization or look for another position within the company? Do you want to remain with your organization? Do you want to keep working in the same industry or perhaps switch? Is this the time to begin an entrepreneurial venture? Are you comfortable with your career trajectory to date? Do you want to stay in the same community or move? Where? What forces out there in the environment do you need to take account of in coming to highly consequential career choices?

Addressing these career questions is difficult, but some structured guidance is available by first identifying the external demands you now experience at work and in your family or private life and then considering carefully how those demands can be met, altered, or otherwise attended to in light of your career anchor. Two exercises are presented on the following pages to help you do this. The first focuses primarily on the work demands you now face or may face in the foreseeable future and the second concerns the ways in which you presently organize your personal and family life alongside your work career and how you would like to do so in the future.

The Role Map: Analyzing Your Present Situation

An analysis of your present situation can be done by first identifying on a role map all the significant and critical people (or groups of people) you know who have important and rather explicit expectations of you. Significant others here are those people whose expectations are of more than passing concern and truly matter to you, expectations you genuinely would like the meet or feel you must meet, including your own (as indicated by your career anchor analysis). List family members, close friends, your boss and subordinates, associations in which you participate, certain work-related peers or groups, and so on. Do not list your entire social network or an exhaustive list of your acquaintances. List just those whose demands and expectations of you currently matter most to you. For an example of a role map, look at Figure 2, and then move on to follow the steps outlined.

Figure 2. Sample Role Map

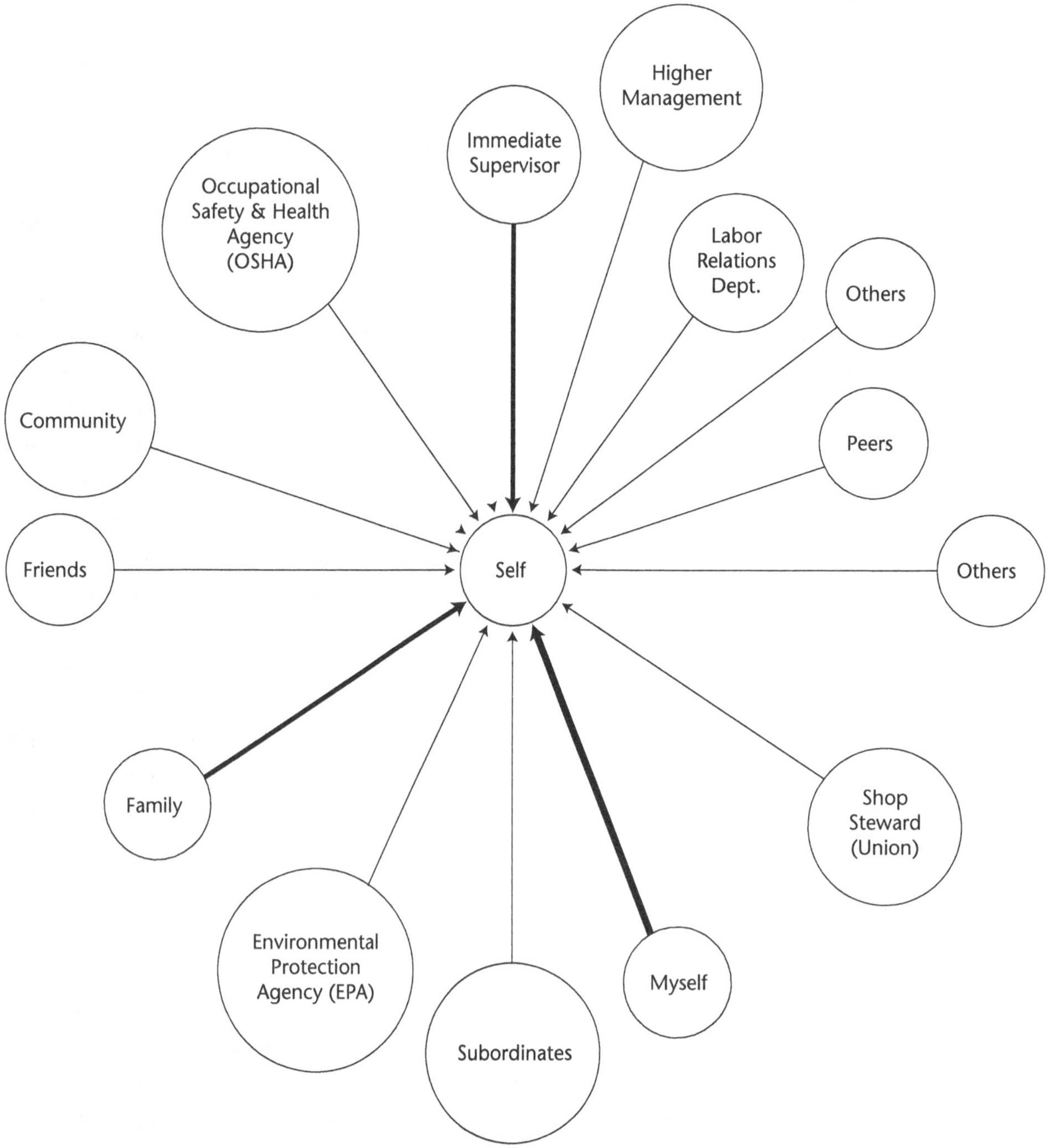

Step 1. Create a Role Map

    a. Using the blank page that follows these instructions, put yourself into the center.

    b. If you are in an organization, put your boss near the top of the paper and draw an arrow toward yourself in the center.

    c. Put your subordinates below you and draw an arrow from each of them toward you in the center.

    d. Continue this process by writing down above, below, to the right, and to the left all of the critical people you can think of who expect something of you in your role. For example, peers in your organization, customers, members of the community, family members including children, parents, and close relatives, close personal friends, and any others. The purpose is to locate all of the people in your "role set" so that you can analyze all of the role expectations to which you have to respond. The width of the various arrows can represent the strength of the relationships and the importance of meeting the expectations of those people.

    e. Draw an arrow from yourself back to yourself because you also have expectations of what you want to accomplish both in and beyond the workplace – such as furthering your education, pursuing particular leisure or side interests such as hobbies and sports, taking part in voluntary or civic activities, meeting your health and fitness targets, and so on.

My Role Map

Step 2. List Major Role Sender Expectations

Once you have identified all the significant people in your role set, make some notes in the space provided as to what the major expectations are of each of the role senders, especially the key role stakeholders, such as your family and the key members of your organization. Try to identify the most essential role expectations, the things that are absolutely critical to your total well-being and life satisfaction.

Step 3. Identify Role Issues and Action Steps

Identifying stakeholder expectations—including your own—likely will have revealed three important issues around roles—ambiguity, overload, and conflict—each of which is described below. Following each description is space for you to record your assessment of the situation and what you might do about it.

Role Ambiguity

For some role senders, you will not be sure what they expect of you. Consider then what you might do to clarify their expectations and put those actions on your "to do" list. For example, you might ask for a meeting to discuss your understanding of your role and invite the role sender to discuss what he or she expects.

Role Overload

The sum total of what everyone expects of you will be much more than you can possibly do. How can you set priorities? Ask yourself whose expectations are most often responded to and whose are most often ignored. Do you communicate your own sense of priorities? For example, you might explicitly communicate to some role senders that you will be late or unable to do what they expect. If you can think of other ways of coping with overload, put the action steps on your "to do" list.

Role Conflict

You will also discover that what some members of your role set expect is in direct conflict with what others expect or what you expect of yourself. Ask yourself how to resolve those conflicts, whether to deny that they exist, compromise by doing a little for each, confront the role sender? Think of action steps you can take to reduce the role conflicts and put those on your "to do" list. For example, if two of your peers expect things of you that are in conflict, consider bringing them together to examine what they expect and how that impacts you.

How Well Is Your Career Anchor Matched to Your Present Job?

Now you can compare what you are looking for in terms of your career anchor with what you have learned about your present job and your role network. Are there major mismatches between your current job and what you are really looking for in terms of career and life satisfaction? You can also use role mapping of this sort to assess possible future kinds of work and, most importantly, to assess your readiness for those imagined work challenges and what you might do to meet them. As a final role map exercise, it may be helpful to again review the key role ambiguities, overloads, and conflicts that you have identified above and, in light of your career anchor, prioritize the action items on your "to do" lists.

What requires your immediate attention? Whose support do you need if an overload problem is to be resolved? How might you clarify (and influence) the expectations others hold of you? If, for instance, your career anchor is pure challenge and the role senders you've identified on your map currently provide little in the way of challenge, what might you do to possibly stretch, prioritize, or restructure your current job to better fit your anchor? How might you let those surrounding you at work—as identified on your role map—know that you are ready to try your hand at more taxing and formidable assignments that test, expand, and strengthen your interests and skills? The fact that all jobs have differing degrees of role ambiguity, overload, and conflict associated with them means that there is always room for shaping the work you do, thus addressing various obstacles and complications that curb your career anchor.

The Work Career and Family/Life Priority Grid: Analyzing Your Present Situation

While it is the case that the kind of work we do and how we do it may well be a major clue to the kind of people we are, the things that interest us, and our sense of self and character, we do not go it alone. All of us have personal lives and roles we play outside the workplace that matter greatly to us. Family life is, of course, one of the most if not the most important in this regard. And whether we are married or not, with or without children, just beginning or ending our work careers, in a close relationship with another, or on our own requires establishing what we come to consider appropriate ways of integrating the various spheres of our lives. Much talk today concerns the difficulty of integrating what we want and can achieve between our careers and what is important to us in our non-work lives. We want to "have a life" as well as a work career, which requires various degrees of accommodation. As the hackneyed phrase goes, few of us on our deathbeds will wish we had spent more time at the office.

It is the case that the time commitment required of managerial and professional employees has escalated in recent years (Jacobs & Gerson, 2004). And, by most measures, professional women—including mothers with young children—are working more than ever (Percheski, 2008). Such trends have an impact on the lives we are able to lead. In combining full-time work and parenting, families in the United States, for example, must make do as best they can, given that there are no national policies supporting affordable daycare, paid parental leave, or work hour regulation. Despite the piecemeal adoption by some companies and a few public agencies of "family friendly" initiatives such as flexible scheduling, maternity and/or paternity leaves, or temporary part-time work, it is the case that many employees avoid taking advantage of such initiatives because they are convinced that to do so would be a "career limiting" move and others in the organization would soon pass them by. Such trends and conditions certainly make it difficult to achieve a satisfying integration of the various spheres of our lives, but they also increase the importance of trying to do so and thinking clearly about the kinds of tradeoffs we can and are willing to make.

To help you sort out your own and your partner's priorities and how you have accommodated them, follow the instructions below to locate yourself on the work/life priority grid based on the work of Lotte Bailyn (2002, 2006) shown in Figure 3. The grid asks you to consider the demands in your daily life that currently have the highest priority.

Your first task is to rate yourself by assessing the priority you now give to your career and family. All of us must decide how to allocate our time, energy, and commitments among employment, family responsibilities, and other activities such as civic engagement and leisure. Ignoring the numbered cells for the moment, place yourself in one of the three priority categories across the top of the grid by putting a checkmark above one of three choices: Career, Equal, or Family/Life. If you check

Figure 3. Work Career and Family/Life Priority Grid

Yourself

		Work Career	Equal	Family/Life
P a r t n e r	**Work Career**	1	2	3
	Equal	4	5	6
	Family/Life	7	8	9

Work Career = More responsibility and commitment for work career than to family and other aspects of your personal life

Equal = Responsibility and commitment equally divided between work career and family and other aspects of your personal life

Family/Life = More responsibility and commitment to family and other aspects of your personal life than to work career

Source: The Work Career and Family/Life Priority Grid was developed by Lotte Bailyn, MIT Sloan School of Management, 2000.

Career, this means you now take more responsibility for and express more commitment to your work career (and external demands) than to the family and other personal and community involvements. If you choose Family, this means you now take more responsibility and express more commitment to your family and other personal involvements than to your work career. If you select Equal, this means you evenly divide your responsibilities and commitments between your family and work career. Family here refers to those people and activities in your personal life that provide you with emotional gratification, such as your spouse or partner, your children, and your extended family; this grouping could also include important avocations and community or religious involvements. For those currently living alone, "family" might be the people and the activities you most care about.

Next, look down to the left side of the grid and specify as best you can how your partner would prioritize the three categories. Check that choice. Is it work or family, or is it equally shared? Here a conversation with your partner is worthwhile, both to check your own judgment about your partner's orientation as well as to double-check the assessment you've made of your own primary orientation. A spouse may well see his or her partner's everyday behavior in a rather different light, and it is important to have a reasonably accurate and agreed-on account of just how work and family commitments are currently undertaken and by whom. If you are now without a partner, you might consider what sort of choice you would like an ideal partner to make (and why).

As the final step, place yourself on the grid by specifying which one of the nine cells intersects with the two priorities you've just checked—your partner's and your own. If you checked Career for yourself and Equal for your partner, you'd fall into Cell 4. If you checked Family for yourself and Equal for your partner, you'd fall into Cell 6. If you checked Career for both, you'd fall into Cell 1. And so on. Circle the number in the cell you've identified as characterizing your current family/work situation. You may also want to consider where you would like to be at some point in the future—three, five, or even ten years ahead—and mark with an arrow the cell that best characterizes that situation. Figure 4 illustrates how your grid may now appear.

Having identified a particular cell—from 1 to 9—that best defines your family/work situation currently—and perhaps at other life stages to come—now think through some of the benefits provided and difficulties encountered within that cell. Importantly, all cells represent both viable and workable arrangements. A satisfying life is possible in any of these nine cells. Each cell, however, presents a different set of problems and challenges, and each has implications for the kinds of career anchors that perhaps best fit the cell. Families of all kinds can make any

Figure 4. Work Career and Family/Life Priority Grid—Completed Sample

Yourself

	✓ Work Career	Equal	Family/Life
Partner Work Career	1	2	3
✓ Equal	(4) ──In 3 years──▶ 5	5	6
Family/Life	7	8	9

Work Career = More responsibility and commitment for work career than to family and other aspects of your personal life

Equal = Responsibility and commitment equally divided between work career and family and other aspects of your personal life

Family/Life = More responsibility and commitment for family and other aspects of your personal life than to work career

Source: The Work Career and Family/Life Priority Grid was developed by Lotte Bailyn, MIT Sloan School of Management, 2000.

of these patterns work, but the difficulties the cells present vary. Consider now what the cells suggest in terms of your work, family, and personal concerns.

Equal Sharing Patterns (Cells 1, 5, 9) reflect a similarity of personal needs and career orientations of both partners. Each cell, however, represents a different life situation.

Cell 1 describes a situation in which both partners are in the midst of high-level, high-involvement careers. Both are rooted and oriented strongly to their respective work lives and the cell might well describe the dual career of a couple who both have strong general manager anchors. This cell is incompatible in significant ways with raising children—particularly young children—or having much of a family-focused or even couple-oriented life. What family life can be had is likely to require considerable planning as well as turning over many household or childcare duties to outsiders in paid employment or to others—perhaps other family members—willing to take on such work. The pattern is probably appropriate for those with high work achievement goals and relatively low needs for intimacy. This pattern is obviously incompatible for those with lifestyle anchors built around family, home, community, or personal interests. The pattern might serve commuting couples well. It probably would work better with couples with autonomy, challenge, and/or technical/functional anchors than those with service or security/stability anchors. Clearly, this pattern works best if the career stage and career success of both partners are similar; if one is too far "ahead" or "behind" the other, incompatibilities may build.

Cell 5 is perhaps the hardest cell of all nine to manage well. This cell contains a very high potential for role conflicts of many sorts and no doubt requires continual and considerable flexibility, negotiation, and compromise on the part of both partners. Reference groups are important since the norms of the groups we identify with help shape what we take to be respectful, equitable, and fair in both our work and personal lives. Reference groups could be our neighbors, circles of friends, parents, the associations we join, work colleagues, and so forth. Your Role Map might help you identify your key reference groups. Indeed, understanding the influence of others on how you commit your time at work and elsewhere is central to managing this pattern well. This is probably the most common pattern for married couples in the United States, since both partners—across all income levels—are likely to work full time. There is, of course, much talk as well, especially among those following managerial and professional careers, about the growth of an equal sharing ethic at home when it comes to performing household and childcare duties. Yet women still do considerably more of this work than men. While those in high-paying jobs can "outsource" some of the housework and childcare, many (if not most) women still face a "second shift" at home. Any of the eight anchors could be located in this cell, although those anchored in autonomy might be somewhat less frazzled by the demands and variability of the pattern.

Cell 9 is hardly compatible with any demanding work career. Work is undertaken primarily to support a lifestyle. Consider those of Gen X or the Millennial generation, some of whom want little to do with establishing a work career resting on long hours, allowing little leisure time in which to travel, spend time with friends, mountain climb or, as they might say, "simply enjoy life." Consider too those whose lives revolve around the full-time care of a permanently disabled child or watching over and providing for aging parents. Lifestyle concerns and interests are of overriding importance. Career progress at work is secondary to life pursuits, whether family or personally oriented. This may well fit some who are fortunate and have independent sources of income, but it is difficult to manage if economic needs and anxieties are high. Those with security and lifestyle anchors may find the cell workable, as may some with service anchors if they are not pulled too far away from hearth and home. Occasionally, entrepreneurial careers are launched by couples as a way of merging their mutual family orientations into a joint venture that allows them to operate on more or less the same schedule, in the same place, and trade off work demands as family needs arise. The cell may, however, involve—on one or both partners' parts—feelings of "failure" where unmet aspirations arising from various career anchor concerns and goals are prominent and be a source of dissatisfaction, guilt, or shame.

Moderately Differentiated Patterns (Cells 2, 4, 6, 8) rest on relatively modest differences between the personal needs and career orientations of partners in the family system. These patterns can accommodate most career anchors, with the exception of lifestyle. The distinguishing characteristic associated with these cells is that one partner is simply less committed to a work career than the other—devoting more time and attention to the family or his or her own non-work interests. In Cells 2 and 4, one partner is dedicated entirely to his or her work career. Both partners may have careers that matter to them, but the intensity with which they are pursued, the commitment they display to them, and the responsibilities they take up differ. One goes all out at work, while the other holds back. Women, for instance, may reduce their commitment to their work careers when their children are young but plan on re-engaging full tilt once their children enter school. A sort of M-shaped career results in which work responsibilities and interests are predominant in, say, the person's twenties and again in his or her forties and fifties but fade in his or her thirties. In many occupations, however, there is a price to be paid for following this pattern. For the partner who adopts the equal role in these cells, a general managerial, technical/functional, or entrepreneurial creativity anchor is likely to be frustrated, at least during those periods in which work commitments are cut back.

These moderately differentiated patterns may also raise issues of competition and comparison between partners over salaries, career progress, status differences, and whether or not one partner feels locked into the equal role for reasons he or she finds difficult to fully embrace. Substantial negotiation (and renegotiation) within families seems a prerequisite to make this pattern work to the satisfaction of both partners.

Cells 2 and 4 are probably a bit harder on family and personal life than Cells 6 and 8 because the commitment to the work career on the part of one partner—and the relative inflexibility of external work demands—may place a disproportionate strain on the other, who is trying to be committed and involved in both his or her work career and family/life. Cells 6 and 8 represent an easing of the commitment to the work career on the part of one partner and, for the other, family and personal life play a dominant role. The danger, of course, is that the equal pattern adopted by one partner may risk his or her career success in the workplace and the economic comfort such success might provide. But as long as both partners consider the cost of success too high in terms of what it might mean for their family and personal lives, the pattern is viable.

Extremely Differentiated Patterns (Cells 3 and 7) are marked by the distinctly non-overlapping roles taken up by partners in any family system. One partner is dedicated to a work career, the other to the family and expects or asks for little in terms of the other's time or energy. If the person who is career-focused is male and his partner female, the pattern is "traditional" and has been met for the most part with wide social acceptance, approval, and support in the past. Over the last thirty or so years, however, women's roles have changed rather dramatically, a reality expressed by the fact that 85 percent of U.S. women now work full-time and do so increasingly in managerial and professional positions. This is one of many reasons these extremely differentiated patterns are on the decline. Among married couples today in the United States, only 13 percent report having a spouse at home who is not in the workforce—a percentage that is down from almost 35 percent some forty years ago (Mishel, Berstein, & Schmidt, 2009).

What characterizes the highly differentiated patterns represented by Cells 3 and 7 is the sharp and distinct partitioning of the partner roles. These patterns work well if they fit the preferences of the people involved and the separation of interests does not grow too distant so that partners become strangers to one another—uninterested and unconcerned with what interests and concerns the other. Bridging efforts are required no doubt to keep the family from drifting apart into entirely separate worlds. It is also the case that role reversals to the traditional pattern are now occurring—although still infrequently—where men take up the responsibility for the care and management of the family while women devote themselves to their work careers. This pattern, since it deviates from established—if shifting—cultural expectations, could result in social isolation and feelings of discomfort and embarrassment for both women and men in such situations. Women in the career role may feel uncomfortable with being the family provider rather than the one who takes care of the family. Women in these non-traditional roles may also feel the pull of the "cult of motherhood" and a sense of guilt may result. Men undertaking the family role may feel both ambivalent and socially awkward about doing so. And this may give way to feelings of shame and resentment at not being a part of a larger world and the recognition that comes from work career accomplishments. Such a reaction, of course, mirrors that of many women situated in a "traditional pattern" who regret not having an independent identity and the general social status and respect associated with work careers.

In terms of career anchors that fit these patterns, almost any anchor aside from lifestyle would seem to work for the partner involved in the work career. If relevant, one way both partners' career anchors might be accommodated is by allowing for a crisscross of orientations at given life stages so that only one partner is in the paid workforce full-time at any given period. The difficulty here is that progress along most career trajectories depends on continuity and experience, and a lengthy time out taken in one's career is typically limiting. Those anchored to autonomy, challenge, and perhaps entrepreneurial creativity may then be the most suited to follow the sort of stop-and-go careers that would characterize the staged switching of work and family responsibilities.

■ ■ ■

You have now completed a career anchor diagnosis, mapped your present work role, and considered the broad pattern that characterizes your current work career and family/life priorities. This should help you identify mismatches between your present job, family, and personal situation, and what you are really looking for in terms of a work career. Moving ahead, you can now think about and plan development activities that reflect the insights you have gained. You may have some jobs in mind for the future and now have a better idea of whether those jobs might suit you and are compatible with your career anchor.

Your own career development depends on your ability to know yourself and your ability to decipher the current (and future) requirements of your job, the career options available to you, and the kind of broader life pattern within which you live. Much may change as you travel through your career, but it is critical to keep in mind how your career anchor, what you most value and do not wish to give up, matches with the possibilities and constraints of the role networks you find yourself connected to both at work and at home. You will find that periodically revisiting the self-assessment, the career history, the role map, and the work career and family/life priority grid will allow you to reflect and, as a result, to make better career and life decisions.

Looking Ahead

THIS SECTION ASKS YOU to consider some of the changes that are occurring in the workplace, in society, and across the globe. Some of these changes seem certain and powerful and likely to alter the career landscape for many of us in particular ways. Other changes seem less so. Sorting such matters out and making accurate and timely predictions in a world that is increasingly volatile, uncertain, and complex is impossible. Yet it is well worth mulling over some of the ideas and trends that we can identify today as a way of preparing for an always uncertain tomorrow.

Globalization and Restructuring

As organizations continue to re-examine their structures and competitive strategies, various kinds of restructuring efforts have been launched. Indeed, we seem to now live in an era in which continual restructuring is generally expected in many, if not most, organizations, be they private, public, or non-governmental. Restructuring is more an art form than a science, occurring in a variety of ways, serving different ends. For the past several decades the emphasis has been on downsizing (or, euphemistically, "rightsizing") based largely on the argument that globalization is a relentless and unceasing force in the world and therefore an organization's ability to compete in such a world depends largely on the stringent control of costs. Innovation, talent, research and development, growth, revenue flows, flexibility, coordination, and continually seeking efficiencies all matter, but only if costs are kept in line and, wherever possible, minimized.

At the societal level, globalization is also taking its toll as countries fearful of losing markets for their goods and services restructure their labor markets to cut wage bills. Massive numbers of jobs that were once regulated to ensure they were full-time, well-paid, and protected from cutbacks have become part-time, poorly paid, and now permit employers to let workers go without restriction. Union membership (and protection) in the United States is now at its lowest point in the past fifty years (Kochan, 2010). All this has led to waves of layoffs and reconfigured organizations such that many jobs have simply disappeared and work has been reallocated and redesigned so that fewer people now perform it.

Consider, too, outsourcing, today a common restructuring practice across most industries—aided if not initiated by dramatic advances in information technologies, the rise of free trade agreements, and the general liberalization or relaxation of governmental restrictions in the economic policies of most nations (still spotty, of course). This puts an even greater strain on domestic labor markets in developed economies that must adjust to progressively cheaper labor available elsewhere, resulting in fewer jobs at home. Such moves are hardly restricted these days to low-skill or back-office work, as so-called "gold collar" jobs in fields such as chip design, medical diagnosis, software development, and many more are also outsourced.

As a result of these more or less macro changes in the world of work, job markets have changed profoundly. Globalization has probably increased the rewards flowing to those highly skilled managers and professionals placed in profitable and surging industries and organizations. But it takes time to reach these ranks. In the United States currently—with the Great Recession of the early 21st Century still at play and unemployment rates still around 8 percent—many people are faltering in their entry into labor markets where weaker job prospects, less security, and greater demands for advanced education (and its steadily rising price) greet them.

More specifically, the gap between the highest and lowest earners in the United States has grown significantly in recent decades. The story is not quite so straightforward because the extremes at both ends of the spectrum demonstrate growth in both wages and jobs. This pattern, labeled "polarization of the job market," is likely to continue at least in the near term, leaving the vast majority of job holders caught in the expanding middle with slim chances of substantial job growth or wage increases (Acemoglu & Autor, 2011; Autor, Katz, & Kearney, 2008).

Making it into the high-earning professional classes is simply more problematic than it once was and seems to require, at a minimum, costly investments in education, lengthy job searches, a greater reliance on personal or family-based ties, longer stretches in entry-level positions, and perhaps a willingness to take on unpaid internships to establish a presence in a given career. It remains to be seen how the recent generations in the U.S. workforce will fare across their careers. Americans, enamored by upward mobility, still believe that their children should have more opportunities and thus do better than their parents, This was taken for granted until the 1980s or so. No more.

What this all means for the concept of career anchors in none too clear. Later starts and slower climbs may disadvantage some of those in the general manager camp, as fewer opportunities to discover and practice management skills will be available. At the same time, the flatter, nimble, and lean team-based organization of the future will require first-rate leadership at all levels. Critical decision-making responsibilities are likely to be picked up at lower levels than they were previously with more "executive responsibility" exercised at all levels in the organization. Those anchored in challenge will find comfort in these organizations, as will those technical/functional managers whose special expertise is in high demand, although this may vary from time to time, firm to firm, and project to project. Those anchored in service may find career opportunities in organizations—perhaps ones they establish themselves—that provide new value-based products or services. Lifestyle and, certainly, security anchors are, however, less likely to be well served in continually restructuring—and cost-conscious—organizations.

Information Technology and Expertise

Globalization and new technologies have loosened the boundaries of organizations, jobs, and roles. At the organizational level, we see in many industries a loosening of the boundaries among suppliers, manufacturers, and customers. By using sophisticated information-technology tools, customers can directly access a company's sales organization, specify in detail what kind of product or service they require, and obtain an immediate price and delivery date sent from the seller's computer. These systems are today ubiquitous. As a result, certain occupational roles such as purchasing agents and sales agents or representatives have changed considerably, and these changes create a chain reaction throughout an organization, requiring a redefinition of other organizational roles in areas such as order processing, marketing, and even design and manufacturing.

At the same time, the computerization and automation of everything from administrative work to complex manufacturing processes makes certain kinds of jobs from secretary to production worker less manual and more conceptual. With the computer, much secretarial work of the routine sort is outdated as the role occupants to whom secretaries once reported take on more and more of the routine work themselves. Even the hallowed task of making appointments has been taken over by managers themselves using all the varieties of smart phones and related handheld multi-functional devices. Secretaries who remain employed take on relatively skilled office-manager-like duties, such as purchasing office supplies and equipment, organizing conferences, and handling internal financial accounts using sophisticated SAP/ERP systems.

Consider also those trained, experienced, and skilled operators who work in automated refineries, nuclear plants, automobile factories, paper mills, and other such organizations who know as much (and maybe more) about running the plant as the managers do. This creates new power relationships. The role of management becomes more ambiguous as managers no longer have the power that comes from knowing things that their subordinates do not. It is especially important for managers in such positions to recognize that the nature of their authority and their relationships to those they nominally supervise have shifted in a number of ways. Workers with high levels of technical skills have come to occupy a much more central position in organizations. And, at least in the United States, the demand for these workers currently (and for the foreseeable future) outpaces supply, thus increasing the power and influence of the technically skilled worker.

At an organizational level, the rapid growth of technology in all fields also means that the number of products and services available is increasing, along with more widely distributed information about these products and services. As competition intensifies, consumers become more demanding and organizations must respond by becoming better able to deliver what customers want faster, in greater variety, and in more places across the globe. A consequence is that organizations will become more complex, differentiated, and require more occupational specialists of different sorts whose efforts must somehow be tied together. Many of these specialists may not be motivated or able to talk to one another, creating special problems of integration of effort.

The highly specialized design engineer or materials scientist working in the research and development area of a company or in manufacturing often has little in common with the financial analyst whose specialty is the management of the firm's investment portfolio or the HR specialist concerned with the most recent interpretation of affirmative action legislation. Yet all these and many other specialists contribute in major ways to the welfare of the total organization and their efforts will have to be managed in such a way that the value each brings to the organization is not diminished or lost.

Such changes would seem to offer more and more opportunities for those anchored in the technical/functional domain while reducing some of the oversight roles and enlarging the integration roles played by general managers. These shifts in the occupational landscape may also favor those with autonomy and challenge anchors, given the likely growth of part-time, contract, and project-to-project work available in technical fields. For those with entrepreneurial anchors, ventures resting on utilizing and/or providing expertise in software development, in biotechnology, in sustainability, and so forth, will have an advantage. The impact on those with service, security, and lifestyle anchors is less clear, however; although all careers are likely to demand more in terms of skills and knowledge than in the past as the link between human capital and career opportunity tightens. Job markets will continue to increase the rewards flowing to the most skilled and credentialed. Yet the time required and the cost of advanced education will put many at a disadvantage, perhaps most of those whose economic resources are limited.

Support and Service Functions

As work—and, more generally, life—becomes technically more complex, more support services are needed. In the workplace, fewer people will occupy operational roles and more people will be needed in knowledge-based service and staff roles supporting the operation. This will create odd organizational dilemmas. For example, the labor cost savings expected from investments in automation and computerized work processes may turn out to be illusionary, as such efforts may more often than not result in a redistribution of the workforce. Fewer operators are needed, but more support services are required. The total cost of the operation may not change all that much. But the kinds of work that are performed change radically and the relationships between groups in the organization change as well. Operators have greater immediate responsibility for doing things right, but the programmers, systems engineers, and maintenance engineers have greater ultimate responsibility to keep the systems up and running—to keep the office computers, billing systems, communication devices, or factory equipment from "going down." Management becomes more a coordinating and liaison function and less a monitoring and control function. Peers in service roles come to be seen as much more central in the help-and-advise or troubleshooting networks than they had been previously.

More broadly, we now live in an economy dominated by the service sectors, with little or no decrease in sight. Most visibly perhaps is the growth in the health services and the ever-growing needs and demands of an increasingly health conscious (and aging) society. Public service jobs in the United States, while shrinking during the recent economic downturn, will no doubt rebound and likely grow in areas such as education, public safety and security, health care, defense, preservation and management of natural resources, job training, and so forth. Consider also the rise of the so-called "third sector" or not-for-profit organizations that will probably continue to increase in both number and influence. Such organizations range from the international variety such as the World Wildlife Foundation or Save the Children to regional and local forms such as those devoted to energy-saving initiatives or poverty intervention programs.

Even within for-profit enterprises, sustainability initiatives, community outreach, or other social responsibility programs may thrive. Concern for the so-called "triple bottom line"—people, planet, profit—animates a good deal of organizational discourse and suggests that an expanded spectrum of values for measuring organizational performance and success may be on the horizon, however controversial it may appear today (Savitz & Weber, 2006).

All this suggests that those anchored by service may have a wider array of possible career choices than at present. Lifestyle anchors tied to social ends may also benefit, although some service jobs said to be "family friendly," such as public school teaching and administration or patient care work in hospitals, may in fact require long and irregular work hours, rigid schedules, and limited if any opportunity to work part-time (all of which may be quite important for those with a lifestyle anchor). General management and technical/functional anchors are in great demand in the service and support sectors and will continue to be so for the foreseeable future. Those anchored in security will no doubt find the increasing need for support and service work welcome, since these job markets are perhaps less precarious and more stable than others. And, as noted earlier, we will probably see an increase in social entrepreneurship as organizations—not-for-profit as well as for-profit—are built to address unmet social needs.

Uncertainty, Anxiety, and Teamwork

As conceptual work increases and job/role boundaries loosen, anxiety levels will increase. People depend on certain levels of predictability and stability. Although we all have needs for creativity and stimulation, we forget that those motives can only operate when there is a baseline of security, stability, and predictability. As organizations face increasing competitive pressures, as jobs become more conceptual, and as the responsibility levels in all jobs increase, we will see stress and anxiety levels increase at all levels of the organization. Formalization and bureaucracy have in the past been a defense against such anxiety, but formalization and bureaucracy are increasingly seen as dirty words, holding back innovation and needed change. Ironically, the kind of work that needs to be done in our current information and knowledge age requires more flexibility and ingenuity, thus making more anxiety an inevitable result.

An increasing role for management will be the containment and working through of anxiety levels. Yet it is not at all clear by what individual or group mechanisms this will occur. When people are anxious, they want to be with others who share their anxieties, and one of the most important functions of groups in organizations is the management of shared anxiety. The increasing emphasis that is being placed on egalitarian groups and teams as fundamental organizing units within organizations may be the result not only of the growing complexity of work but of the growing anxiety levels attending work.

At the same time, information technology now makes it possible for members of such groups and teams to be physically in different locations. This may well dampen the anxiety reduction role groups and teams play in organizations, perhaps even increasing the anxiety that goes with the work. One certainty is that the increasing use of virtual teams in organizations heightens the requirement to build and develop trusting relationships within such groups so they can work together comfortably and productively. This is a task that managers have found difficult, even in the old office-bound work environment that provided considerable opportunities for face-to-face gatherings of formal and informal sorts.

The concept of sociotechnical systems has been promulgated for many decades, but as we project ahead, it would appear that it becomes a more important concept than ever. One cannot separate the technical elements of a job from the social elements, as the difficulties of managing virtual teams makes clear. The sharing of information, knowledge of critical interdependencies, provision of social and emotional support, cultivation of effective communication skills, and the widespread commitment to commonly held goals allow technical systems to operate smoothly and take advantage of the talents of the engineers, designers, and operators involved. And as technical work becomes more complex and sophisticated, it will require more teamwork, thus increasing the importance of understanding sociotechnical systems.

Some observers suggest that the relational skills women possess because of their different socialization experiences—in childhood, in school, in the workplace—may provide them an advantage when it comes to leading and managing teams. Relational skills typically refer to the willingness to listen closely to others, being approachable, communicating clearly, demonstrating empathy and patience, and so on. The data here, however, are far more speculative and impressionistic than conclusive, nor is it clear what relational skills in particular lead to success as either team players or team leaders in specific work worlds. Perhaps more to the point is the fact that women studied to date display the same range of career anchors as men and thus, presumably, the same range of talents, motives, and values. The distribution of anchors varies by time and place, and some careers remain culturally coded as "male" or "female," although rigid distinctions between the two are breaking down, a consequence of changing attitudes and thirty years of equal opportunity and anti-sex discrimination legislation in the United States.

What we do know is that employment levels among college-educated women in professional and managerial occupations are increasing such that women have more career opportunities than ever before. That their respective careers are likely to involve increased amounts of teamwork seems inevitable, whatever the skills and interests of the women moving into these work worlds.

One obvious implication of the increasing importance and growing emphasis on teamwork in organizations is that the ability to effectively manage groups of all sorts—a subtle skill to be sure—will be required of all managers, regardless of their specific career anchors. This may be a bit more difficult for those with technical/functional and challenge anchors, who may not have either the empathy or understanding required to effectively lead teams made up of members with diverse backgrounds, skills, and interests (or the desire to gain such skills). And the more diverse these teams, the more difficult it may be. One thing that seems apparent is that the ability to manage groups of all sizes and types will be increasingly the mark of a general manager whose social and emotional competences will be tested repeatedly.

For those with lifestyle, service, or security anchors, their ability to manage teams well probably depends more on whether the larger organizational context of their work satisfies their anchors than on the specific demands of that work. Entrepreneurs are notorious at not handling group and team management tasks well—except in the start-up phases of an organization, when they are typically surrounded by those like-minded few who share their energy, excitement, and goal. Those with an autonomy anchor may be quite skilled in managing groups effectively, as many project managers have demonstrated. But managing teams of diverse and sometimes distant members may require the sort of time, travel, and meeting commitments that cannot be avoided or delegated, and thus conflict with the independence sought by those with autonomy anchors.

New Organizational Forms

In the process of restructuring, organizations are (a) re-examining and trimming their hierarchical structures, particularly in the middle ranks; (b) moving toward flatter organizations; (c) relying more on coordination mechanisms other than hierarchy; (d) "empowering" their employees in various ways; and (e) becoming more flexible in regard to projects they undertake (and abandon) as well as the people they employ (growing in fat times and retrenching in lean). In the flat, flexible, networked, project-based organization of the future, power and authority will rotate among different project leaders, and individual project members will have to coordinate their own activities across a number of projects with different leaders. Operational authority will shift rapidly from one project leader to another, and individual employees may find themselves matrixed with several bosses—with uncertain or ambiguous authority claims—simultaneously. At the same time, as knowledge and information are more widely distributed, employees will become de facto empowered because they will increasingly know things that their bosses will not know.

However, hierarchy is fairly intrinsic to human systems. One of the most useful functions of hierarchy lies in the resolution of conflicts. As disputes arise at one level, they are settled at another. So we will probably not see the abandonment of hierarchical structures so much as a re-emphasis in some of the chain of command functions and a decline in others. In particular, the coordination of powerful project groups, divisions, and other organizational units will continue to require effective leadership and hierarchy to avoid the inevitable political power struggles that arise in an intergroup and inter-organizational context. For example, broad hierarchical categories, such as civil service grades or degrees of partnership in a law firm or levels of professorial rank in a university, may continue to serve broad career-advancement functions, but may not be a good guide as to who will have high status within the organization or operational authority over a given task, project, or area. Respect for people and the amount of influence they exert will have more to do with their reputations and task performance than with their formal rank, and hierarchy will increasingly be viewed as a necessary adjunct to organizational life, rather than its prime principle.

Power and authority will derive from what a given person knows and what skills he or she has demonstrated. But since conceptual knowledge is largely invisible, the opportunities for misperception or conflicting perception of who knows what and who should be respected for what will increase, making the exercise of authority and influence at all levels much more problematic. This in turn will not only increase anxiety levels in organizations but put a premium on social skills such as negotiation, conflict management, and coalition building, thus highlighting the importance of building trusting relationships across various kinds of organizational boundaries. How such relationships can be built with or without regular face-to-face contact will be among the main challenges of the future (Schein, 2009, 2010).

Careers in organizations in which hierarchies have been thinned, structures flattened, and flexibility emphasized will be of a protean sort. The traditional definition of a successful manager as one who climbs the corporate ladder the highest in the shortest amount of time generally peaking between the ages of forty-five and fifty-five fits a mid-20th Century male characterization, a period when people had children in their twenties, stayed in one job and organization throughout their careers, and retired at sixty-five (and died at seventy-one). This definition makes little sense today for a number of reasons, some structural, some not. Life expectancy for people in their twenties is around eighty, and when in good health we can work to seventy-five or more—and, given the rising cost of living, shrinking retirement benefits, and dismantling of societal safety nets, this may become a necessity.

We have children later now or not at all. Many of us expect to live on two incomes, not one. We enter the workforce later and we expect to have multiple jobs (if not multiple careers) throughout our work lives. Rewards for loyalty and long service are unexpected and sometimes seen to violate the performance-based incentive systems being put into place by many organizations. The career is—as we have continually pointed out in this workbook—no longer a straight climb up (or off) the corporate ladder, but rather a combination of climbs, lateral moves, periods spent out of the workforce, and even planned or unplanned descents. What Benko and Weisberg (2007) call a "lattice career" is now relatively common, and we expect it to become even more so in the future.

Several career anchor implications are apparent. There will be fewer well-established routes to the top of an organization from the inside, thus reducing the value of organization-specific skills and knowledge. Those with general management anchors will move increasingly across organizations, and perhaps industries, looking more for increased responsibilities and job scope than for rank. Technical/functional types will be even more concerned than at present with keeping abreast of developments in their respective fields to avoid being bypassed and hence supplanted by those who are younger and sharper—and often cheaper. Those with autonomy and challenge anchors may find the new order welcome in that their comfort with flexibility serves them well.

Entrepreneurs too may find the growing emphasis on flexibility welcome, given the loose organizational structure so characteristic of start-ups. Security, service, and lifestyle anchors may be less well-suited for careers marked by high degrees of variability, unpredictability, and vulnerability—worlds where employment guarantees are a thing of the past and one is judged solely by those performance metrics currently in fashion; where projects undertaken for the greater good are dependent solely on the good will of transient leaders who are here today and gone tomorrow; where hard-earned skills can become obsolete overnight; and where flexibility means never being beyond the reach of the organization or clients, often requiring prolonged periods of 24/7 effort impervious to the personal needs of employees.

Interdependence and Collaboration

In order to produce increasingly complex products and services effectively over a period of time, the work of many subunits (and subspecialties) of the organization must be aligned and coordinated. All subunits are in one way or another dependent on the work of other subunits, and such interdependency can break down. If, for example, the financial department does not manage the company's cash supply adequately, there is less opportunity to invest in new product development or increase manufacturing capacity. If an engineering design sacrifices some elements of quality for low cost, the result may be customer complaints, a lowered company reputation, and a subsequent inability of the company to borrow money for capital expansion. In this sense, engineering and finance are highly interdependent, even though each may be highly specialized and neither may interact with the other directly.

Sequential, as opposed to simultaneous, interdependence is the more common situation. The engineering department cannot design a product or service if the research and development (R&D) group has not done a good job providing a concept or prototype; in turn, manufacturing cannot build the product if engineering has put forth an unbuildable design; and sales and marketing cannot do their jobs if they have poor products or services to sell. R&D cannot be effective if marketing has not provided them a clear picture of future customer needs or possibilities, and the process innovations occurring in manufacturing will often influence both marketing and engineering in terms of the types of products that are thought feasible.

And we know that so-called lead customers or lead users strongly influence— or should strongly influence—innovation by feeding back to the producing organization ideas for how products and services could be improved (Von Hipple, 2005). While the "clock speed" of industries differ in terms of their respective (and highly interdependent) development-to-production-to-sales cycles, competitive advantage typically goes to the swiftest organizations within an industry (Fine, 1998).

But as we look ahead, simultaneous interdependence is becoming both more common and more difficult. Tasks such as performing a complex surgical operation require the coordination of several specialists who may come from different occupational and cultural units. These types of interdependencies have always existed within and between organizations, but as specialization increases, so does interdependence because the final product or service is more complex and more vulnerable to any of its multiple parts malfunctioning. Nowhere is this clearer than in computer products or services. The hardware and software have to be designed properly in the first place and then implemented by a variety of specialists, including, crucially, those who staff the growing number of support and help lines making sure that customers can actually use (and continue to use) the computer product or service they purchased.

Each organizational subunit and specialty develops something of its own subculture—specialized jargon, ways of working together, rules of thumb, certain ways of seeing the world and analyzing problems, standards of evaluation, and so on. Such subcultures are often more responsive to their own technical communities than to their organizations as represented by general management. But these subcultures as part of the larger organization are interdependent and must work together, and it is becoming more and more evident that persistent competition and rivalry among subcultures is divisive and potentially destructive. Teamwork and collaborative/cooperative relationships across subcultural segments are increasingly touted as necessary, providing the kind of social glue that holds organizations together and contributes to their success. This is, however, a view that often runs counter to the external marketplace philosophy that regards self-determination and competition—individual or collective—as good, a view that perhaps has more sway in the United States than elsewhere.

Yet, in the face of this apparent cultural contradiction, collaboration and teamwork are increasingly seen to be necessary adaptations within organizations, even if inter-organizational relations continue to be highly competitive. Indeed, a good deal of recent research shows just how critical team learning, knowledge transfer, and relational coordination within and across subunits are to successful organizational performance (Edmundson, 2012; Gittell, 2009).

How collaboration is achieved depends less on political or top-down strategies or mandates than on the practical and operational necessities experienced by those doing the work. Increased collaboration is rarely achieved by corporate degree or centralized planning but by decentralizing and providing more information of the sort that permits various units to coordinate among themselves. What Malone (2004) calls "the future of work" embodies these very characteristics. However, for self-managed coordination to occur, not only must information be widely available and shared, but all those involved must be able to decipher their roles within the broader system since the same information can be framed and interpreted in many different ways by those in different subcultures. For collaboration to work with interdependent but culturally diverse groups, common frames of reference must be established, and this may require that organizational members take part in far more intercultural, group, and team activities than is the case at present (Schein, 2009, 2010).

This move toward interdependence and collaboration poses a dilemma for managers whose own careers developed in a dog-eat-dog, competitive environment and who simply do not have the will or interpersonal competences to redesign their organizational processes to be more supportive of collaborative relations and cross-cultural understandings. Many managers today pay lip service to "teamwork" but their day-to-day style sends clear signals to others that they do not really understand or support the concept, with the predictable result that the "team" does not function as a team at all. Unfortunately, both the manager and his or her subordinates may draw the erroneous conclusion that it is the teamwork concept that is at fault, rather than locating the problem in their own failure to understand and create conditions that would allow collaborative relationships to emerge.

Because collaboration requires information to flow laterally between technical specialists, some companies are putting product development and sales and marketing departments closer to one another geographically, thus informally stimulating direct contact between those in the differing units. Open office designs explicitly seek to enable contacts that promote knowledge transfer as well as increased understanding of others' beyond one's own immediate work group. Increasingly, the client, the salesperson, and the marketing specialist in a complex industry such as electronics or health care all probably know more about the technical side of the business than the general manager, and therefore must be brought into direct interaction with designers and engineers if a viable product or service is to result. Lateral structures of many different types—project teams, task forces, matrix management, ad hoc committees, cross-functional groups, informal groups, unauthorized skunk works—become more common with increased complexity and environmental uncertainty.

Of course, lateral structures work only if people are not discouraged from or punished for talking and working with people outside their own chains of command (an unwritten rule that is no doubt still enforced in many organizational settings). Yet, given the increasingly shrill cry from insiders and outsiders alike to break up the "silo mentality" in organizations both large and small, we expect to see more and more forms of lateral (bridging) structures develop in the coming years.

It is probably the case that those with technical/functional and challenge anchors will have the most difficulty adapting to increasing interdependency. Those with a strong technical/functional bent are almost by definition carriers of subcultural values and assumptions, including the inclination to see others who are not similarly trained and skilled as less competent, perhaps in need of enlightenment. The engineers that Scott Adams of *Dilbert* fame parodies as individualistic, fiercely independent, and smart yet socially clueless are hardly ideal team players. Those oriented primarily toward personal challenge may also find building collaborative relationships at work a stretch, a task requiring the sort of openness that might dull their competitive edge. And the intense teamwork required to manage interdependencies may not suit those with autonomy anchors since the pace, schedule, and workload one undertakes is less an individual than a collective matter.

Sharing information and working closely with diverse others may come easier for those with service, lifestyle, and security anchors for whom being at the top of one's game or putting one's technical acuity to use are secondary. Seeking a common purpose, helping others (and the reciprocity such exchanges generate), and doing one's part, whatever it may be, to ensure the organization survives and prospers may all lend themselves well to leading diverse teams in uncertain environments and avoid the sometimes personal and parochial interests associated with other anchors. Successful entrepreneurs know that they cannot go it alone; having others who check and balance one's weaknesses is critical. Building a heterogeneous leadership team comprised of those who are not shy in voicing their views while listening carefully to others seems a necessity if entrepreneurial ventures are to succeed. Talented general managers have long been aware of the importance of interdependencies and know quite well the difficulty of integrating the highly differentiated organizations of today. These challenges are growing, thus increasing the need for those who can effectively bring those from different parts of the organization together.

Work, Self, and Family

There once was a time when one could write of a common value system in America. Erving Goffman, for example, with tongue only partially in cheek, wrote in 1963 that "the only completely unblushing male in America is the young, married, employed, protestant, white, urban, northeastern, heterosexual, father, college educated, of normal weight, above average in height, of good complexion, and with a recent history of sports." Such words conjure up a highly standardized and prejudiced society in which one either did or did not fit the proper mold. The professional and managerial worlds of this imagined period were made up of "organization men" who, in gray flannel suits, shuffled off each day to large but tidy and rule-bound corporate bureaucracies to work 9 a.m. to 5 p.m. on whatever dull task was required. Vestiges of this stock image remain, but most of us would regard this portrait as both misleading historically and downright archaic by today's standards. If anything, what was once a worry about the tyranny of a uniform, conformist culture has been replaced by doubt as to whether there is any shared culture at all.

The reasons for this turnabout are complex. But we do know that people generally are placing less value on traditional concepts such as unquestioned organizational loyalty and the acceptance of authority based on formal position, age, or seniority and are placing more value on individualism and individual rights vis-à-vis the large organization. Increasingly, people are asking that the tasks they are asked to perform provide them with a sense of meaning and an opportunity to express their talents. Increasingly, people are demanding that the rights of individuals be protected, especially if they are in danger of being discriminated against on some arbitrary basis, such as gender, sexual preference, race, age, religion, or ethnicity. Increasingly, people want to have some voice in decisions that directly affect them at work and at home. Progress in all these areas over the past forty or fifty years is notable, although it has come unevenly, in fits and starts, and, for many, at far too slow a pace.

We know also that people are placing less value on work or career as a total life concern and less value on promotion per se or hierarchical movement within an organization as the sole measure of "success" in life. Today, much talk is given over to how we can lead a balanced life in which career, family, and self-development all receive their fair share of attention. It is then arguably the case that "success" for many of us is increasingly being defined in terms of the full use of our talents and contributing not only to our work organization, but to family, community, and self as well.

Less value is being placed on traditional male and female gender roles with respect both to work and family. Gender-role stereotypes are breaking down, thus opening up the range of career choices for both men and women. People are also questioning the value placed on economic growth and, even in hard times, interest is still apparent in conserving and protecting the quality of the environment in which we live. Indeed, assessing not only the economic but also the environmental and social impact of technology has become a major activity in society. What "progress" means, however, is up for grabs. Nowhere is this more apparent than in the bitter debates surrounding both the causes and consequences of the distribution of wealth in society.

We have become a more divided and fragmented nation. Value changes and conflicts have created a situation in which the incentives and rewards offered to and by the different segments of our society are increasingly diverse and less integrated. We see this in the "generation gap." In organizations, the gap pits relatively well-placed older managers or employees who embrace a "protestant work ethic" against younger workers who question arbitrary authority, restrictive personnel practices and policies, meaningless work, and even long-established corporate goals and means. Older workers see the younger generation as unambitious, unwilling to pursue careers that require dedication and entail the surrender of personal interests and time. Younger workers see their older colleagues as trapped by a narrow definition of success, more or less married to their jobs, and not having much of a life outside the workplace.

Part of this, as we have said, reflects labor market shifts and persistent high unemployment and underemployment rates, particularly among youth. Good jobs are harder to find and keep and depend increasingly on attaining the sorts of skills higher education—including post-graduate studies—is thought to provide. Certainly, parents and adult children are worried about what the future holds, about whether this Millennial generation, for example, will equal, much less surpass, the occupational status and income of the Boomer generation. Part of this is also personal. Some younger people want nothing to do with sixty- or seventy-hour workweeks, constant travel, self-promotion, frequent relocations, close supervision, and persistent career anxieties. Some older workers, too, have begun to question the traditional success ethic, and examples of managers refusing promotions or geographic moves are relatively easy to find. Some "retire on the job" to pursue family activities or off-the-job pursuits, and some have even resigned from high-potential careers to pursue "second careers" seen to be more challenging and rewarding by criteria other than rank or income.

It is easy, however, to exaggerate the degree to which such "opting out" is occurring in society. The standard corporate executive's or politician's claim that he or she is "stepping down to devote more time to the family" is viewed by most of us as cover for something else. How could anyone voluntarily give up power and position for the joys of parenthood? This cynical view is both ironic and maddening, given the ritual commitments we routinely make to "family values." Male leaders are still often praised for having sacrificed their personal lives for public or corporate service. Those who choose families are either disbelieved or are viewed as "unprofessional."

Much has been written in the past twenty or so years about the benefits and promises of such policies as flexible work schedules, maternity and paternity leaves, working from home or telecommuting, part-time work careers, and so on. Yet the demands of most workplaces remain predicated on the concept of the workers as "male" and relatively free of personal responsibilities. Most men work full-time, regardless of their family situations, leaving women (who may also work full-time) the "hard choices," including not having children, having fewer children, not working, working less, or working the same as men and coming up with private solutions that allow for both high levels of employment and some sort of family life. Men still seem more likely to choose a job at the cost to the family, while women are more likely to choose the family at the cost of a job. But this gap seems to be shrinking. What we have seen to date among those on professional and managerial career tracks are smaller families aided increasingly by paid outside help and a plethora of private solutions to various work/life integration dilemmas. The much-talked-about "opt out revolution" of women in professional and managerial fields leaving the labor force for motherhood has not occurred. In fact, employment levels and full-time work among college-educated women in these fields continues to increase, even among mothers of young children (Percheski, 2008).

In general, the social organization of work or family life has changed little in the past thirty or forty years, although men are now slightly more active at home with childcare and household duties. A result is that work-family difficulties have grown more pervasive since dual-career couples are now the norm. Most working women experience a real time bind due to competing demands of work and family life and combine these roles often only by curtailing sleep and leisure activities (Hochschild, 1997; Perlow, 2012). This issue is unlikely to go away since both the opportunity costs for not working and the time demands associated with well-paid occupations continue to rise (Jacobs & Gerson, 2004). Beyond a financial penalty, there is another price typically paid for stepping off a career track for a time by taking a leave, going part-time, or taking advantage of a particular flexible time option.

The penalty is that those who choose to reduce their work involvement, even if only temporarily, are typically seen by others at work as less committed to the organization (or their professions) than those who continue to work full-time—a stigma that is often career damaging if not career breaking. A good example of this is a recent hospital study in the Boston area where a policy change that reduced work hours for surgical residents from 120 hours per week to eighty was fiercely resisted by most of those men and women to whom it would apply in two of the three hospitals studied for reasons having much to do with the perceived damage that following the new policy would have on their future careers (Kellogg, 2011). A similar stigma can even attach itself to those who do not take a leave, go part-time, or reduce their hours of work but choose only to telecommute or work from home in those organizations where time in the office or face time is taken as a critical sign of commitment. Some women pay the price and take advantage of these policies; men, for the most part, do not.

It is important to note that most flexible work arrangements are set up on a case-by-case basis as individual or one-off accommodations (and exceptions) to workplace norms (Bailyn, 2011). As such, they do not address the problems of aligning the needs of the workplace with the various (and evolving) needs of the workforce. While some general flexible policies have been adopted by organizations around issues such as schedules, hours, and assignments, these modest shifts (for example, the four-day, ten-hour work week; flexible starting and quitting times; rotating shifts; and so on) do not address the larger career questions surrounding work role expectations, quality of assignments, pace for promotion, and what it might mean in terms of career development for one to be "off-track" for a spell.

Even in the most reputedly "family friendly" firms, the policies on the books to aid employees are on the order of providing childcare referral services, on-site dry cleaning and banking services, relocation and travel aid, permanent casual dress standards, and, in a few cases, on-site childcare. For the most part, the flexible work arrangements offered currently to managerial and professional employees by most organizations do little to ease the work/life integration difficulties many face.

What we have seen, however, is a creeping commercialization of family and personal life (Hochschild, 2012; Turco, 2012). The number of paid specialists who provide, for example, child care, elder care, and domestic services such as shopping, cleaning, and cooking are on the rise. These fields owe their growth to an individual's willingness to pay someone else to do what he or she once did him- or herself or did with the free help and support of family and friends. For those putting in long and exhausting hours on the job and living without much support from family and friends, such services are a necessity and will no doubt continue to be in demand.

The implications for the future of these work, family, and life considerations are mixed across the eight career anchors. Those anchored in lifestyle are unlikely to see much happening that will ease their ability to combine work, family, and personal concerns. While value swings at the societal level or major structural changes in workplace policies are possible, there is little evidence that this is actually occurring. Those with entrepreneurial anchors are perhaps little affected here because achieving work/life balance, however nice, is not a primary concern. On the other hand, entrepreneurs may find more opportunities for creating new forms of organization that deal with these issues more creatively. Those with general manager anchors may find moving ahead somewhat more problematic given that they are more likely than in the past to be in partnerships with those who are also career-oriented and therefore equally busy. Managing two careers simultaneously is usually more difficult than managing one and, for the general management anchored, the tradeoffs required may stall or otherwise affect the career trajectory one wants to realize.

For those anchored in security or service, the future may be less problematic than the past or present, as definitions for what "success" means in society are likely to be less narrow and uniform and the single-minded pursuit of a work career less expected. Challenge and autonomy anchors may also be well-served in the future, as both types are presumably fairly comfortable moving in and out of the workplace and hence will perhaps be able to balance work, self, and family concerns sequentially throughout a career.

Implications for Your Career Development

WE HAVE PROVIDED THIS extended analysis and set of predictions to enable you to think clearly about your own career future and how you will need to plan for your own development. Things are changing in both predictable and unpredictable ways. You will most of all need a clear concept of *who you are* with respect to work, family, and personal needs.

To help you in this analysis, we have provided a set of items that cover a broad range of motives, values, and competencies for you to use as a kind of checklist of possible areas of career development. Given your personal and family situation, you can add further items to help you consider future priorities and required accommodations.

Assessment of Future Requirements

Instructions: Rate yourself on each of the items below. A "1" means you do not possess that motive, competence, or value to any degree, while a "4" means you possess it to a great degree. For each item, provide two ratings. Put a *circle* around the number that represents where you think you are now. Put a *cross* through the number where you think you ought to be, given your present situation and your thoughts for the future. Try to be honest with yourself because this is not a test but a way of identifying your own strengths, weaknesses, and developmental needs.

A. Motives and Values	Low		High	
1. My desire to get a job done, my need for accomplishment	1	2	3	4
2. My commitment to my organization and its mission	1	2	3	4
3. My career aspirations and ambitions	1	2	3	4
4. My degree of involvement with my career	1	2	3	4
5. My desire for high levels of responsibility	1	2	3	4
6. My desire to take risks	1	2	3	4
7. My desire to make tough decisions	1	2	3	4
8. My desire to work with and through people	1	2	3	4
9. My desire to exercise power and authority	1	2	3	4
10. My desire to monitor and supervise the activities of others	1	2	3	4
11. My desire to delegate and help others to succeed	1	2	3	4
12. My desire to function as a general manager free of functional and technical constraints	1	2	3	4
13. My desire to work collaboratively rather than competitively with others	1	2	3	4
14. My desire to learn	1	2	3	4
15. My desire to take risks, even if that leads to errors	1	2	3	4

B. Analytical Abilities and Skills

	Low			High
16. My ability to identify problems in complex, ambiguous situations	1	2	3	4
17. My ability to sense quickly what information is needed in relation to a complex problem	1	2	3	4
18. My ability to obtain needed information from others	1	2	3	4
19. My ability to assess the validity of information that I have not gathered myself	1	2	3	4
20. My ability to learn quickly from experience	1	2	3	4
21. My ability to detect errors in my own actions	1	2	3	4
22. My flexibility, my ability to think of and implement different solutions for different kinds of problems	1	2	3	4
23. My creativity, ingenuity	1	2	3	4
24. My breadth of perspective and insight into a wide variety of situations	1	2	3	4
25. My degree of insight into myself (strengths and weaknesses)	1	2	3	4

C. Interpersonal and Group Skills

	Low			High
26. My ability to develop open and trusting relationships with peers	1	2	3	4
27. My ability to develop open and trusting relationships with superiors	1	2	3	4
28. My ability to develop open and trusting relationships with subordinates	1	2	3	4
29. My ability to listen to others in an understanding way	1	2	3	4
30. My ability to communicate my own thoughts and ideas clearly and persuasively	1	2	3	4
31. My ability to communicate my feelings clearly	1	2	3	4
32. My ability to influence people over whom I have no direct control	1	2	3	4
33. My ability to influence my peers	1	2	3	4

34. My ability to influence my superiors	1	2	3	4
35. My ability to influence my subordinates	1	2	3	4
36. My ability to diagnose complex interpersonal and group situations	1	2	3	4
37. My ability to develop processes that ensure high-quality decisions without having to make the decisions myself	1	2	3	4
38. My ability to develop a climate of collaboration and teamwork	1	2	3	4
39. My ability to design processes to facilitate intergroup and inter-functional coordination	1	2	3	4
40. My ability to create a climate of growth and development for my subordinates	1	2	3	4

D. Emotional Abilities and Skills

	Low		High	
41. My ability to make up my own mind without relying on the opinions of others	1	2	3	4
42. My ability to share power with others	1	2	3	4
43. My ability to tolerate and acknowledge errors	1	2	3	4
44. My degree of tolerance for ambiguity and uncertainty	1	2	3	4
45. My ability to take risks, to pursue a course of action, even if it may produce negative consequences	1	2	3	4
46. My ability to pursue a course of action, even if it makes me anxious and uncomfortable	1	2	3	4
47. My ability to confront and work through conflict situations, rather than suppressing or avoiding them	1	2	3	4
48. My ability to keep going after an experience of failure	1	2	3	4
49. My ability to confront my stakeholders if there is role ambiguity, overload, or conflict	1	2	3	4
50. My ability to continue to function in the face of continued environmental turbulence	1	2	3	4

List below other items that occur to you and that apply to your family and personal development needs:

_____

_____

_____

_____

_____

_____

_____

_____

_____

_____

_____

_____

_____

_____

_____

_____

_____

_____

_____

_____

_____

_____

_____

_____

_____

_____

_____

_____

_____

_____

_____

_____

_____

_____

_____

_____

Next Steps

FIRST LOOK AT THOSE ITEMS FROM THE SELF-ASSESSMENT you just took for which there is the greatest discrepancy between your present rating and where you feel you should be. For each area for which you feel there is a significant discrepancy, figure out a development plan for yourself or figure out how to restructure your job so that your present capacity will be sufficient to do the job.

If you conclude that you must restructure your job, think that through in terms of renegotiating with the requisite stakeholders and ensure that the new expectations are realistic, both from your point of view and their points of view.

List below the various developmental or restructuring actions you plan to take and keep this list as a point of reference to be reviewed at various times in the future.

Item Number: _____

Developmental Plan:

Item Number: _____

Developmental Plan:

Item Number: _____
Developmental Plan:

Item Number: _____
Developmental Plan:

Item Number: _____
Developmental Plan:

Given all of the plans you've made, what are the next steps that you will take? Try to be specific and give a time frame for each step.

Step 1 and Time Table:

Step 2 and Time Table:

Step 3 and Time Table:

Step 4 and Time Table:

In conclusion, your own career development will depend on your ability to know yourself and to decipher the requirements of future jobs and career options. Think especially of how your career anchor, what you value and do not wish to give up, matches with the possibilities and constraints of future jobs.

References and Additional Reading

Acemoglu, D., & Autor, D.H. (2011). Skills, tasks and technologies: Implications for employment and earnings. *Handbook of Labor Economics, 4*, 10043–1171.

Arthur, M.B., Inkson, K., & Pringle, J.K. (1999). *The new careers.* Thousand Oaks, CA: Sage.

Arthur, M.B., & Rousseau, D.M. (Eds.). (1996). *The boundaryless career.* New York: Oxford.

Autor, D.H., Katz, L.F., & Kearney, M.S. (2008). Trends in U,S. wage inequality: Revising the revisionists. *The Review of Economics and Statistics, 90*(2), 300–323.

Bailyn, L. (1978). Accommodation of work to family. In R. Rapoport & R.N. Rapoport (Eds.), *Working couples.* New York: Harper & Row.

Bailyn, L. (1992). Changing the conditions of work: Implications for career development. In D.H. Montross & C.J. Schinkman (Eds.), *Career development in the 1990s: Theory and practice.* Springfield, IL: Thomas.

Bailyn, L. (2002). *Beyond work-family balance: Advancing gender equity and workplace performance.* San Francisco: Jossey-Bass.

Bailyn, L. (2011). *Breaking the mold: Redesigning work for productive and satisfying lives* (2nd ed.). Ithaca, NY: Cornell University Press.

Barley, S.R., & Kunda, G. (2006). *Gurus, hired guns, and warm bodies: Itinerant experts in the knowledge economy.* Princeton, NJ: Princeton University Press.

Barth, T.J. (1993). Career anchor theory. *Review of Public Personnel Administration, 13*, 27–42.

Benko, C., & Weisberg, A. (2007). *Mass career customization.* Boston: Harvard Business School Press.

Bianchi, S.M., Casper, L.M., & King, R.B. (Eds.). (2005). *Work, family, health, and well-being.* Mahwah, NJ: Lawrence Erlbaum Associates.

Briscoe, J.P., & Hall, D.T. (2006). The interplay of boundaryless and protean career attitudes: Combinations and implications. *Journal of Vocational Behavior, 69*, 4–18.

Briscoe, J.P., Hall, D.T., & Mayrhofer, W. (2011). *Careers around the world: Individual and contextual perspectives*. London: Routledge.

Crepeau, R.G., Crook, C.W., Goslar, M.D., & McMurtney, M.E. (1992). Career anchors of information systems personnel. *Journal of Management Information Systems, 9*, 145–160.

Davis, S.M., & Davidson, B. (1991). *2020 vision*. New York: Simon and Schuster.

Derr, C.B. (1986). *Managing the new careerists*. San Francisco: Jossey-Bass.

Durcan, J., & Oates, D. (1996). *Career paths for the 21st century*. London: Century Business Press.

Edmundson, A.C. (2012). *Teaming: How organizations learn, innovate, and compete in the knowledge economy*. San Francisco: Jossey-Bass.

Farber, H.S. (2010). Job loss and the decline in job security in the United States. In K. Abraham, J. Spletzer, & M. Harper (Eds.), *Labor in the new economy*. Chicago: University of Chicago Press.

Fine, C. (1999). *Clockspeed: Winning industry control in the age of temporary advantage*. New York: Basic Books.

Gittell, J.H. (2009). *High performance healthcare: Using the power of relationships to achieve high performance*. New York: McGraw-Hill.

Goffman, E. (1963). *Stigma*. New York: Simon and Schuster.

Gunz, H., & Peiperl, M. (Eds.). (2007). *Handbook of career studies*. Thousand Oaks, CA: Sage.

Hall, D.T. (2002). *Careers in and out of organization*. Thousand Oaks, CA: Sage.

Harrington, B., & Hall, D.T. (2007). *Career management and work-life integration: Using self-assessment to navigate contemporary careers*. Thousand Oaks, CA: Sage.

Harrison, B. (1997). *Lean and mean: Why large corporations will continue to dominate the global economy*. New York: Guilford Press.

Higgins, M.C. (2005) *Career imprints*. San Francisco: Jossey-Bass.

Ho, K. (2009). *Liquidated: An ethnography of Wall Street*. Durham, NC: Duke University Press.

Hochschild, A.R. (1997). *The time bind: When work becomes home and home becomes work*. New York: Holt.

Hochschild, A.R. (2012). *The outsourced self: Intimate life in market times*. New York: Metropolitan Books.

Ibarra, H. (2003). *Working identity: Unconventional strategies for reinventing your career*. Boston: Harvard Business School Press.

Jacobs, J., & Gerson, K. (2004). *The time divide: Work, family and gender inequality*. Cambridge, MA: Harvard University Press.

Kellogg, K. (2011). *Challenging operations: Medical reform and resistance in hospitals*. Chicago: University of Chicago Press.

Khurana, R. (2002). *Searching for the corporate savior: The irrational quest for charismatic CEOs*. Princeton, NJ: Princeton University Press.

Klinenberg, E. (2012). *Going solo: The extraordinary rise and surprising appeal of living alone*. New York: Penguin.

Kochan, T.A. (2010). *Resolving America's human capital paradox: A proposal for a jobs compact*. Paper posted on the website of the Employment Policy Research Network. Available: www .employmentpolicy.org.

Kossek, E., & Lambert, S. (Eds.). (2005). *Work and life integration: Cultural and individual perspectives*. Mahwah, NJ: Lawrence Erlbaum Associates.

Malone, T.W. (2004). *The future of work: How the new order of business will shape your organization, your management style, and your life*. Boston: Harvard Business School Press.

Mishel, L., Bermstein, J., & Shierhotz, H. (2009). *The state of working America, 2008–2009*. Ithaca, NY: Cornell University Press.

Newman, K.S. (2012). *The accordion family: Boomerang kids, anxious parents, and the private toll of global competition*. Boston: Beacon Press.

Nordvik, H. (1991). Work activity and career goals in Holland's and Schein's theories of vocational personalities and career anchors. *Journal of Vocational Behavior, 38*, 165–178.

Nordvik, H. (1996). Relationships between Holland's vocational typology, Schein's career anchors, and Myers-Briggs' types. *Journal of Occupational and Organizational Psychology, 69*, 263–275.

Osterman, P. (2009). *The truth about middle managers: Who they are, how they work, how they matter*. Boston: Harvard Business School Press.

Percheski, C. (2008, June). Opting out? Cohort differences in professional women's employment rates from 1960 to 2005. *American Sociological Review, 73*(3), 497–517.

Perlow, L.A. (2012). *Sleeping with your smartphone: How to break the 24/7 habit and change the way you work*. Boston: Harvard Business School Press.

Poelmans, S.A.Y. (Ed.). (2005). *Work and family: An international research perspective*. Mahwah, NJ: Lawrence Erlbaum Associates.

Reitman, F., & Schneer, J.A. (2003). The promised path: A longitudinal study of managerial career. *Journal of Managerial Psychology, 18*, 60–75.

Savitz, A.W., & Weber, K. (2006). *The triple bottom line: How today's best-run companies are achieving economic, social, and environmental success*. San Francisco: Jossey-Bass.

Schein, E.H. (1971). The individual, the organization, and the career: A conceptual scheme. *Journal of Applied Behavioral Science, 7,* 401–426.

Schein, E.H. (1975). How career anchors hold executives to their career paths. *Personnel, 52,* 11–24.

Schein, E.H. (1977). Career anchors and career paths: A panel study of management school graduates. In J. Van Maanen (Ed.), *Organizational careers: Some new perspectives.* Hoboken, NJ: John Wiley & Sons.

Schein, E.H. (1978). *Career dynamics: Matching individual and organizational needs.* Reading, MA: Addison-Wesley.

Schein, E.H. (1987). Individuals and careers. In J. Lorsch (Ed.), *Handbook of organizational behavior.* Englewood Cliffs, NJ: Prentice-Hall.

Schein, E.H. (1996). Career anchors revisited: Implications for career development in the 21st century. *Academy of Management Executive, 10,* 80–88.

Schein, E.H. (2010). *Organizational culture and leadership* (4th ed.). San Francisco: Jossey-Bass.

Sennett, R. (2006). *The culture of the new capitalism.* New Haven, CT: Yale University Press.

Turco, C. (2012). Difficult decoupling: Employee resistance to the commercialization of personal settings. *American Sociological Review, 118*(2), 380—419.

U.S. Census Bureau. (2010). *Married couple family groups by labor force status of both spouses.* Washington, DC: Author: Available: www.bls.gov/population/socdemo/hh-fam.

Van Maanen, J., & Schein, E.H. (1977). Career development. In J.R. Hackman & J.L. Suttle (Eds.), *Improving life at work.* Santa Monica, CA: Goodyear Publishing.

Yarnall, J. (1998). Career anchors: Results of an organization study in the UK. *Career Development International, 3,* 55–61.

About the Authors

Edgar H. Schein was educated at the University of Chicago; at Stanford University, where he received a master's degree in psychology; and at Harvard University, where he received his Ph.D. in social psychology in 1952. He is Sloan Fellows Professor of Management Emeritus at MIT's Sloan School of Management. Previously, he was chief of the Social Psychology Section of the Walter Reed Army Institute of Research while serving in the U.S. Army as Captain from 1952 to 1956. He joined MIT's Sloan School of Management in 1956 and was made a professor of organizational psychology and management in 1964. From 1968 to 1971, Dr. Schein was the undergraduate planning professor for MIT, and in 1972 he became the chairman of the Organization Studies Group of the MIT Sloan School, a position he held until 1982. He was honored in 1978 when he was named the Sloan Fellows Professor of Management, a Chair he held until 1990.

Dr. Schein has been a prolific researcher, writer, teacher, and consultant. Besides his numerous articles in professional journals, he has authored fourteen books, including *Organizational Psychology* (3rd ed., 1980), *Career Dynamics* (1978), *Organizational Culture and Leadership* (1985, 1992, 2010), *Process Consultation Vol. 1 and Vol. 2* (1969, 1987, 1988), *Process Consultation Revisited* (1999), and *The Corporate Culture Survival Guide* (2009). Dr. Schein wrote a cultural analysis of the Singapore Economic Development Board entitled *Strategic Pragmatism* (MIT Press, 1996) and has published an extended case analysis of the rise and fall of Digital Equipment Corporation entitled *DEC Is Dead; Long Live DEC: The Lasting Legacy of Digital Equipment Corporation* (Berrett-Koehler, 2003). He was co-editor with the late Richard Beckhard of the Addison-Wesley Series on Organization Development, which has published over thirty titles since its inception in 1969. He has consulted extensively on career development and corporate culture in the United States and abroad.

Dr. Schein received the Lifetime Achievement Award in Workplace Learning and Performance from the American Society of Training Directors (2000), the Everett Cherington Hughes Award for Career Scholarship from the Careers Division of the Academy of Management (2000), the Marion Gislason Award for Leadership in Executive Development from the BU School of Management Executive Development Roundtable (2002), the Lifetime Achievement Award as Scholar/Practitioner from the Academy of Management (2009), and the Lifetime Achievement Award from the International Leadership Association (2012).

John Van Maanen works within the fields of organization behavior and theory. He is an ethnographer of organizations ranging in type from police organizations to educational institutions as well as a variety of business firms. He has taught in the Sloan School of Management at MIT since 1972. In 1988 he was named the Erwin Schell Professor, a Chair he still holds. He has been a visiting professor at Yale University, University of Surrey, and INSEAD in France. His undergraduate education was at the California State University at Long Beach, and he earned his Ph.D. from the University of California at Irvine.

Dr. Van Maanen has published a number of works in the general area of occupational and organizational sociology. Cultural descriptions figure prominently in his studies of the work worlds of patrol officers on city streets in the United States, police detectives and their guv'nors in London, fishermen in the North Atlantic, MBA students at MIT and Harvard Business School, and park operatives in the Sistine Chapel of Fakery, Disneyland (here and abroad). He is the author and editor of numerous books, including *Organizational Careers* (1977), *Policing: A View from the Street* (1978), *Tales of the Field* (University of Chicago Press, 2nd ed., 2011), *Qualitative Studies of Organizations* (1999), and *Organizational Transformations and Information Technology* (with Joanne Yates, 2001).

Dr. Van Maanen is a member of the American Sociological Association and a Fellow of the American Association of Applied Anthropology. He has served on the editorial boards of a variety of journals, including *Administrative Science Quarterly, Human Organizations, Journal of Contemporary Ethnography, Human Relations* and, most recently, *Journal of Organizational Ethnography.*. He has worked with numerous public and private organizations in North America, Europe, and Asia, including, recently, Li and Fung, BP, Moller-Maersk, U.S. Internal Revenue Service, Lafarge, Warburg Dillon Read, and Hong Kong University. He was the faculty chair of the Sloan Fellows Program at MIT from 1994 to 2000 and the faculty chair of the Organization Studies Group (1995 to 2000, 2003 to 2008).